Parzival ♦ Gawain

I0880089

Chrysalis Productions Presents
Parsifal
or the Legend of the Holy Grail
A play by Arthur Maximilian Miller
Saturday, April 25th, 7:30pm
Sunday, April 26th, 3:00pm
Angelico Hall, Dominican College
San Rafael, CA
Tickets: Adults $15, Children $12
For Tickets Call: 415-389-9816

PARZIVAL ♦ GAWAIN

two plays drawn from

Der Gral

by Arthur Maximilian Miller

Translated and edited by
Daniel Joseph Polikoff

RSCP

Translated with permission of the
Arthur-Maximilian-Miller-Stiftung,
Augsburg, Germany.

Cover art: Iris Sullivan

ISBN 0-945803-67-2

The content of this book represents the view of the author and should in no way be taken as the official opinion or policy of Rudolf Steiner College or Rudolf Steiner College Press.

Book orders may be made through
Rudolf Steiner College Bookstore
Tel. 916-961-8729, Fax 916-961-3032,
E-mail: bookstore@steinercollege.edu.

Rudolf Steiner College Press
9200 Fair Oaks Boulevard
Fair Oaks, CA 95628, U.S.A.

This book is dedicated with love and gratitude to my parents

Alexander and Barbara Polikoff

two true chivalric spirits

Contents

Foreword

One of the most important qualities of the Grail legend is its mutability. Since the Middle Ages, audiences have enjoyed these legends again and again in various forms. The past few decades in America have seen numerous tellings and retellings of the tale in both literary and cinematic medium—from high brow to low brow—from the serious to comedic. One can make the argument that, just as classical culture rested upon the foundation of Homer, the culture of the modern age of secular humanism rests upon the legend of the Grail.

It is a distinct characteristic of this legend (and the age to which it speaks) that many voices participate in the conversation of its continued re-creation. There is no one "canonical text" of the Legend of the Holy Grail; there is no one indisputable touchstone of absolute scriptural authority; rather, the text of the Grail legend is in a continual process of dying, metamorphosis, and rebirth. With every fresh generation in the West, new voices return to tell the tale in distinctive ways.

Arthur Maximilian Miller's contribution, in this edited translation by poet and scholar Daniel Joseph Polikoff, exemplifies once more the Grail's persistent and living reality. Poets, writers, and minstrels have long understood that one of the paths to the Grail's holy mysteries opens through the practice and discipline of art. By telling and retelling the tale time and again, poets, artists, and musicians find their way to the Magic Mountain. And, by undertaking this pilgrimage in the craft of poetry, poets honor the reality of the spirit while renewing the power of mythology for audiences and themselves.

The Grail is not merely an object contextualized by history. It is a living fact of the spirit whose efficacy and promise persist into present times. Audiences who hear the tale told and retold time and again, and poets who master their art to rehearse the tale, are joined in the celebration of a mystery. It is a mystery that defines the character, meaning, and destiny of the free individual in his or her relation to the spirit. It is a mystery that holds the key to the purpose, destiny, and challenge of the culture and civilization of the West.

University of California, Davis *Bruce T. Donehower*

Preface

Soon after moving to the San Francisco Bay Area in 1997, I had the good fortune to meet Karen Rivers. At that time, Karen was recruiting interested persons for a community theatre production of Parzival. The script in her possession consisted of excerpts of nine scenes drawn from *Der Gral* (The Grail) by Arthur Maximilian Miller, a little known German author. This excerpted script was originally employed by the Stuttgart eurythmy group for their performance of *Parzival*. (Eurythmy is a dance/movement art introduced by Rudolf Steiner.)

Karen originally hoped that the Miller excerpts might serve as a playscript, but, as the cast began to study the text, it soon became evident that it was too fragmentary. Karen knew that I had translated German literature, and as the time to begin our weekly rehearsals approached, she procured a full copy of Miller's (out of print) original. Putting the tome in my hands, she asked if I might find time to fill out our seed-text a bit as the need arose. Little did I realize that this enterprise would consume the better part of my creative energies for the next several months! Yet I never regretted the task, for intensive labor on *Der Gral* amply confirmed my initial impression: Miller's was a work of the highest order, combining philosophic profundity with literary excellence. I quickly came to regard the opportunity to work with the text so closely and in so living a fashion as an honor, even a sort of gift of the Grail.

Arthur Maximilian Miller was born on June 16, 1901 in Mindelheim, in the Schwabian part of Germany. The son of a merchant, the young Miller became a teacher before dedicating himself to a distinguished literary career, composing works in High German as well as his local Schwabian dialect. In his forties, Miller commenced work on *Der Gral* as a spiritual antidote to the horrors of the Second World War. Miller finally brought the work (which he himself considered his masterpiece) to completion nearly forty years later.

Der Gral, composed in the blank verse typical of classical German drama, runs over 350 pages. While presented in dramatic form, it is primarily a literary text not suitable for theatrical performance. Adapting the monumental work for the stage required severe editing; not only were vast tracts of text entirely omitted, but those sections and speeches that did find their way into the playscript often required radical pruning to serve dramatic pacing.

The division of the material into two distinct, though integrally related, plays is another consequence of the challenge of transforming epic matter into living theatre, and one that merits a few words of explanation.

The original production of *Parzival* included within it the first meeting of Parzival and Gawain in the woods near Plimözel (featured on this book's cover) as well as Gawain's spectacular triumph in the Castle of Marvels. In reviewing the play, I felt that, without more of Gawain's story, this latter scene seemed out of place. I originally considered trying to include more of the Gawain material in the Parzival script, but this would have resulted in an oversized work that could in no wise be presented in a single evening. What finally decided me in favor of the two-play division, however, was my sense that the quality and pacing of the Parzival and Gawain material was different enough that the central character of each might shine more brightly if presented as the hero of his own play. Gawain is placed first because, although he enters the larger story well into the action, the successful completion of Gawain's quest is the prerequisite for Parzival's. Gawain's attainment in the relational domain of soul (consummated by his marriage to Orgeluse and the reintegration of the social world centered around King Arthur) precedes and prepares Parzival's realization of the redeeming power of the human spirit.

So far as I know, these plays represent the first full-length dramatic but non-operatic version of Parzival. It is worth noting that Wagner's famous opera, while superb in its own right, does conflate Parzival's and Gawain's quests in a manner that obscures important spiritual themes.

Under Karen Rivers' direction, the early version of *Parzival*—complete with original music by Marcia Burchard—premiered successfully in San Rafael, California, in 1998. Karen originally intended to mount a production of *Gawain* the following year. While various circumstances precluded that, the staged reading given by the San Francisco Playwrights' Center in 1999 greatly helped the refining of this playscript. At the time of this writing, *Gawain* awaits its first full production.

The tradition of Grail literature is tremendously rich and accomplished. Miller's work stands squarely in the German line; the plot of *Der Gral* follows that of Wolfram von Eschenbach's *Parzival* fairly closely. What, then, sets Miller's account of the Grail apart from others—especially Wolfram's timeless classic? What in particular recommends this text to the modern reader?

First of all, the author of *Der Gral* is himself a master craftsman. Miller's language is consistently tensile and colorful; his is a truly poetic drama that often achieves lyric beauty even in the midst of the action. In this connection, it is well to remember that Wolfram's own *Parzival* is an epic poem composed in Middle High German tetrameter couplets. While English narrative translations may preserve a great deal of the significance of Wolfram's original, much of its poetical character is inevitably lost in translation. Miller's writing cannot make good that loss, but it is revivifying to read of the Grail in the freshly minted coin of Miller's own dramatic poetry. If I have done my job well, poetry is not the main thing lost in this translation.

At its best, Miller's original imagery conjures symbolism that, at every step of the way, amplifies the meaning of events. When, for instance, Parzival leaves Herzeleide to seek his fortune as a knight, Herzeleide blesses the shoes that will bear him onward with these words:

> Be covered, you defenseless soles.
> It is the earth, my child, that you tread.
> 'Til today, I carried you, but now
> bless these soles that carry you further on your way.

A world of meaning is contained in this simple speech/gesture: the transition from a child carried—physically and spiritually—by his mother, to the young man and aspiring human being whose ground and destiny now becomes (mother-) Earth. Miller's writing is filled with such gems so that the texture of his work, like the armor of Parzival's half-brother Feirifis, shines with the luster of hidden wisdom.

And then there is the drama. Miller's chosen form—especially in this theatrical edition—makes both the feeling lives of the characters and the compelling action more immediately available to us than does Wolfram's denser narrative. In the opening scene of *Parzival*, Herzeleide's deep grief for her dead husband, as well as her love for her child, sing out of her words, gestures, and palpable stage presence. It is one thing to read of Parzival's devastation after his initial failure at the Grail castle, another to see and hear him on stage as he shrinks at his cousin Sigune's (and later, of course, the hideous Kundry's) curse:

Sigune:

Penance, yes, do penance,
when all's past and gone. Your penance
won't win a hair of healing. You lost
your head when you lost your heart. All's in vain,
all foolishness, fool! You can ask me a thousand questions—
I'll say no more!

Parzival:

Will you cast me
into darkness, into deserted waste?

Sigune:

You yourself
are night, and waste.

Such dramatic immediacy will be especially welcome to readers who find their patience tested by Wolfram's sometimes elaborately detailed epic, but even Wolfram devotees may find such theatre stirring—even revelatory.

This matter of portrayal of the characters' inner lives transcends form, and in fact has as much if not more to do with Miller's period than with his genre. Naturally enough, the consciousness that pervades these (20th century) plays is distinctly more modern than Wolfram's. For instance, listen to the way in which Itonje images her dawning memory of childhood:

> I was stolen from my father's house
> as a child, and every trace of memory
> sunk as in the blackness of a well
> but now the distant images climb
> up the long dark shaft. . .

The very fact that Itonje thinks in such terms evinces a mode of subjectivity foreign to Wolfram, yet second nature to the modern individual heir (consciously or not) to Romantic and Depth Psychological traditions.

But Miller does not merely give us modern figures in medieval dress. Without betraying the genius that lives in his mythic sources, Miller animates the figures of Grail legend in a way that probes the psycho-spiritual depths of modern consciousness. His prescience in this regard is evident, for instance, in his handling of gender roles. The archetypal differences between the masculine and feminine so strongly marked in medieval chivalric culture lives on in Miller, yet with a distinctly modern twist. The Duchess Orgeluse throws down the gauntlet of the battle of the sexes with sentiments (if not idiom) reminiscent of contemporary radical feminism:

> Is woman, then, to you, but an object
> of desire, a kind of booty stalked like a hind
> so that your coward-spear might pierce it through?
> You are masters of our bodies—how is that?
> . . . We are surrendered, helpless, to your will?
> No, noble hero, . . .
> I—know it—am the vengeance of my sex,
> which your wickedness shames each day and hour.
> You have chosen her, so drink the cup
> she offers you!

When Gawain accepts that challenge (I will drink it, mistress / drain it to the dregs; call me a fool / if that bitter bottom does not shimmer with gold), we are plunged more deeply still into the heart of riddles that vex modern men and women struggling with the division of the sexes. I'll leave the reader to wrestle with Miller's own—in some ways conservative, in some ways truly radical—symbolic resolutions.

It is interesting to note, in fact, that some of the most striking differences between Miller's and Wolfram's treatments emerge in their portrayals of certain feminine characters. That the sorcerer Klingsohr and the blacksmith Trebuchet appear as full-fledged characters (not, as in Wolfram, figures known only through the mouths of others) certainly adds zest and dimension to Miller's drama; nonetheless, the difference in quality that imbues his portrayal of Antikonie and Bene may be more deeply indicative of the distinctive tone and character of his writing. In Wolfram's *Parzival*, Gawain's encounter with Antikonie emphasizes the former's character as "a light lover" and Antikonie is little more than a foil for the impetuous hero's romantic foibles. While this register is present in Miller, the beautifully lyrical love discourse that unfolds between Gawain and Antikonie reveals psychological and philosophical depths unique to Miller:

Antikonie:

What you, sir, as one who's nameless, ask
finds answer through another who's without name.
And would it then be strange, if that answer
must bear witness to what is forever nameless?
If I love you? Do you ask in sport? . . .
O sir, remember, that in a woman's heart
every jest turns fast to earnest thought,
and beneath the light blue mirror of the lake,
which laughingly reflects the image of the shore,
the stone of your question quickly sinks to darkness
in its depths.

Indeed, in this dramatic version, Antikonie emerges as such a powerful and sympathetic character that the reader will likely feel Gawain's abandonment of her especially keenly, and even wonder when this hero will finally leave the shrewish Orgeluse to return to this maiden who appears flawed only by her flawlessness.

Perhaps even more significantly, Bene—the Ferryman's daughter who, in Wolfram, appears more or less a simple girl—possesses a deeply mystical character in Miller. (The Ferryman is also a far more sagacious character than his counterpart in Wolfram.) When, in a moment of communion with the half-dreaming Gawain, Bene says: "Twelve stars it is, so over, so under / the sea," I take that cryptic figure to imply that the wisdom of the heavens (symbolized by the zodiac) is "sunk" or received into the (waters of) the psyche. That figure, I feel, may in some wise symbolize the peculiar turn of Miller's genius: his version of the legend is one that works to absorb the wisdom of the Grail ever more deeply, ever more intimately into the very element of the modern soul.

Miller's *Der Gral*, then, is more than a dramatic retelling of the Grail story; it is a mystery play, an esoteric text in its own right. In this connection, it is worth noting that Miller's writing reveals the influence, not only of Wolfram, but of more contemporary luminaries as well, most particularly Rudolf Steiner. Those familiar with Steiner's work will undoubtedly notice a few moments in these plays that draw directly on Steiner's tenets (for instance, the ninefold division of spiritual hierarchy spoken of by the angel choir in *Parziva*l). More importantly, the epic vision of the nature and destiny of the human being that pervades and shapes *Der Gral* exhibits a profound kinship with Steiner's. Steiner called his teaching

Anthroposophy (*Anthropos-Sophia*, the wisdom of the human being). Near the end of *Gawain*, Parzival utters a phrase that echoes Steiner's founding inspiration:

> The human being! Then let there be
> the human being!

And the final words of *Parzival* recall Steiner's (neo-Emersonian and esoteric Christian) doctrine of Self:

> Your light transforms all Death to Life
> Thus saith the Word: I am.

Despite his deep knowledge of Steiner's teachings, Miller declined to call himself an anthroposophist. Instead, as I learned in a private conversation with Robert Powell, he preferred to style himself, first and foremost, "a servant of the Word." Indeed, what most impresses and breathes through *Der Gral* is the degree to which Miller has made his literary and spiritual sources his own, and how consummately he has reforged the Grail (s)word in the flame of his own inspiration, in the fire of his own art. In the beautiful body of its language, in the deep soul of its characters, in the transcendent wisdom that informs its spirit, *Der Gral* is truly a worthy heir of the great Grail tradition, a masterpiece that deserves wider audience. In this work of translation and theatrical adaptation, I have sought to make its light shine into the (English speaking) world—a world in dire need of the healing force of the Grail.

May the Word do its work; may the Offer be accepted; may Love and Peace come to reign on Earth.

Daniel J. Polikoff
May 2003

Music: Though it was not possible to print the music composed for the Chrysalis production of *Parzival* in this book, those interested in it are encouraged to contact Marcia Burchard, Music Department, Dominican University, 50 Acacia Avenue, San Rafael, CA 94901 (Tel. 415-257-1341). Marcia has not yet composed music for *Gawain*, but again, those interested should contact her.

There are a number of instances in *Parzival* in which a song that does not appear as such in Miller's original is interpolated into the text. These cases are obvious in that the lyrics of such songs always repeat lines spoken in the text.

Stage directions: Some of Miller's stage notes (especially setting descriptions) are elaborate. These are given in full for evocative effect; they clearly need not be taken as precise stage instructions.

Acknowledgments

This book would not have come to be without the inspiration and effort of many. Robert Powell was instrumental in providing the Miller text, in making contact with the Miller Foundation in order to secure translation rights, and supporting the project in other crucial material and spiritual ways. Karen Rivers ignited the the entire project: special thanks for her inspired and tireless work as director of Chrysalis Productions' staging of *Parzival* and her invaluable colleagueship. Thanks as well to Marcia Burchard for her likewise indefatigable work on the musical end of *Parzival*. The San Rafael production of *Parzival* was real community theatre, and grateful acknowledgment is made to all the cast members who bravely put up with a constantly changing script; as well as to the dedicated stage hands, parents, and spouses that made the performances possible.

Thanks to the San Francisco Playwrights' Center for the staged reading that helped make *Gawain* a reality, to Iris Sullivan for the beautiful art work for the cover of this book; to Bruce Donehower and Betty Staley for their contributions; and to the helpful minds and hands at Rudolf Steiner College Press.

Finally, the author would like to gratefully acknowledge the generosity of the Arthur-Maximilian-Miller-Stiftung for granting free permission for this edited translation of Miller's *Der Gral*. Heartfelt thanks as well to the Sophia Foundation of North America and to Barbara Garland Polikoff for the financial support that helped make publication possible.

GAWAIN

In Quest of Love

Dramatis Personae

King Arthur	
Gawain	Arthur's nephew
Galogandres	Landgrave of Shanphanzun in Avalon
Iwanet	Gawain's page
Vergulacht	King of Shanphanzun in Avalon
Knight	in Vergulacht's retinue
Antikonie	Vergulacht's sister
Teudares	nobleman, counselor to Vergulacht
Farmers	commonfolk in Vergulacht's domain
Orgeluse	Duchess of Logrois
Lady	Urians' beloved
Urians	wounded knight
Malcreature	a malformed man-creature
Ferryman	
Bene	ferryman's daughter
Klingsohr	Master of the Castle of Marvels
Elemental Spirits	
Arnive	captive queen in the Castle of Marvels
Castle Maidens	captives in the Castle of Marvels
Itonje	one of the maidens, Gawain's sister
Giromelans	Guardian of the Laurel (Tree of Life)
Angels	
Parzival	Grail-seeker
Priest(ess)	

ACT I: Galogandres

Scene 1 King Arthur's Tent at Dawn

Arthur, who has been awake through the night, has fallen asleep at a table. His mien expresses deep distress. On the table, near his head, a candle burns; near the candle is his crown. Gawain enters and kneels near the king.

Arthur (*waking*):

Who kneels and murmurs here? Gawain! Stand up!
What means this? Why do I find you in arms
before the break of day?

Gawain:

My noble uncle,
my King, and my Master, I am come
to request my leave of you.

Arthur:

You too, nephew, will leave me?

Gawain:

What is my light, since Parzival's went out?
It is in vain: I can stay no longer.

Arthur:

Where will you go?

Gawain:

After him. He rides
towards the abyss. Perhaps I can still catch
and tear him from it.

Arthur:

You—him?

Gawain:

If one voice reach him
in the wilderness, where no human breath
bears word or message to his ear. . .
What is the use of all we further do
if Parzival is lost? I must seek him!

Arthur:

I would not have earned the right to wear
this crown upon my head, if I did not say:
Gawain, you speak the truth.

Gawain:

Then let me go.

Arthur:

Before you do, ask yourself once more
if there be no stain upon your honor,
no taint, no spot—for the littlest lack
augurs ruin in such a work as this.

Gawain:

The test is passed. You saw me kneel. My heart
gave me leave to go.

Arthur (*looking long at him*):

Then let us bid farewell!

(*Gawain nears Arthur. At this moment Galogandres enters.*)

Galogandres:

Where is King Arthur? Where is Gawain?

Gawain:

Here meet you both, impatient warrior,
who enters the tent of the most noble King
without the least sign of courteous greeting.

Galogandres (*to Arthur*):

I offer honor's greetings to you, great hero
whose far-flung fame the wandering minstrels sing.
I offer you friendship, and high praise, I
who am come from Avalon, at behest
of Vergulacht, its noble king, for I
am Galogandres, landgrave and protector
of shining Shanphanzun.

Arthur:

A proud name you bear, and well-renowned.
Be welcome here! Put off your heavy arms.

Galogandres:

I will not ungirdle this, my sword, nor lift
this helmet from off my whitened head. For know:
I do not come in peace; these arms mean war.

(*to Gawain*)

To you, I offer hate and shame, and all
the ill deserved by a villainous head.
For while the light of virtue seems to shine
sun-like, from those smooth features,
evil shadows your still youthful heart,
the worm of malice swells within your breast,
and all posterity shall abhor the very sounding
of your name.

Gawain:

Stop!

Galogandres:

By no means! Before the countenance
of this most virtuous king, who so oft
has stood in judgment on good and evil deeds,
I accuse you of a hidden act
of murder: you took the life of my master,
the father of my own beloved king.
He was found in a swamp in the forest,
his life cut short by the hand of a boyish knave.

Gawain:

Pardon, sir, you speak as if in dream.
Of all this you tell of, I know nothing.

Galogandres:

Good! Perfect your own dishonor, deny
the horrid practice you secretly perform.
But know—like chanticleer upon his roost—
I will announce it to the entire world
unless, before a moon has passed, you come
armed, to our castle, so these our swords
may then decide whether right lives with you,
you counterfeit, or him, for whom I stand.
You'll have safe conduct to the ring of battle—
so much this raised hand assures in pledge.

Gawain:

If snow did not lie thick upon your brow,
I would here, by my king's board, tear
this sword from its sheath, that the slander
you have spoken might stick in your own throat.
And yet—I've been admonished, and so will fit
myself to your designs, denying Gawain,
whose hand's as closely bonded to his sword
as helmet is to head. Upon thy oath,
that assures safe escort! Go hence, and know:
I'll not fail your challenge.

Arthur:

No, here the last word belongs to the king.
I will not suffer you to meet him on the ground
of such foolish suspicion.
Truth, like the light of the sun,
will soon bring forth its own revelation.
We need not anticipate its radiant notice
with our weapons' wild and hasty force.

Galogandres:

Truth reveals itself to the heart,
and yet will oft require the deed of man as mirror
wherein to show its undistorted countenance.
When truth itself calls to action,
it befits men to listen, and obey.

Gawain:

My uncle, let me go! The stain of slander
I'll wash from me, be it with the blood
of the man who lent it such spiteful tongue.
I gave my word, and will not take it back.
(*to Galogandres*)
Within a month, at Shanphanzun, in arms.

Galogandres:

If no vengeful bolt of lightning
snatch you from off this earth,
we meet again where these, my words, will turn
to swords. (*leaves*)

Arthur:

Upon you, too, the somber
curse of fate? I know you are not guilty,
and yet . . . O woe, if your young locks, too,
wed the bloody dust!

Gawain:

No! That will heaven not allow, noble King.
The Tree of Life would not so senselessly
shake its fruit into oblivion's false lap.
(*to himself*)
A curse on Parzival, a curse on me!
(*to Arthur*)
Live well! I am called, and so—ride!

ACT II Antikonie

Scene 1 A Forest Clearing

Iwanet:

Where are we?

Gawain:

Would that I knew, Iwanet!
And yet I think—*not* in Avalon.
Still worse—the winding of this wood
has so confused my sense, I do not know
in what direction Shanphanzun should lie.

Iwanet:

We've chased our tails in this thick forest
for weeks on end.

Gawain:

The track of time—that too,
I've lost. Can you say, how many days
have passed since we left King Arthur 's court?

Iwanet:

Let me reckon it, sir. Is't possible?
Our time is out. A month is spent; today's
the last to appear for battle in Shanphanzun.

Gawain:

What cursed luck! They'll think me a rogue
—a dishonorable coward—since I so shamefully
broke my promise without good ground or cause.
Where, shining Shanphanzun, are you hiding?

Iwanet:

Wait, sir. Look, where it flashes
through the branches there! A kingly procession
rides through the woods.

Gawain:

Hold, they draw
slowly near to us. I think that he
who trots so splendidly in the glow of youth

must be a king or prince. That puts us
in new want; we cannot ask his name or rank
if he himself does not freely tell them.

Iwanet:

The signs that ornament the banners and clothes
are strange to us; they will not give us news.

(*King Vergulacht enters with his followers, all in armor.*)

Vergulacht (*to a knight*):

This is not it; we've not yet found the place.
We must still ride a stretch through the forest.
Know you the stranger?

Knight:

No. He comes, I think, from some distant land
and seems lost here.

Vergulacht:

A noble hero,
I trust—in form and bearing without fault,
his proud features poured from virtue's mold.
I like him well.

Knight:

He greets us.

Vergulacht:

We'll answer him.
Come, let's hasten to him!

Gawain:

Noble sovereign—

Vergulacht:

Welcome, dear sir,
I see that in these woods you've lost your way—
—know not where you stand— and I— forgive me—
will not tell it you. For if you seek
adventure, know, the nameless is most high.
Therefore, nought of names. Instead, let us,

two strangers, draw near each other with true
and unlocked hearts, and see if confidence—
yea, love itself—may not bloom
from our initial greeting. Be my guest.
Beyond this wood, you'll find an open plain
close by mountainous cliffs—there stands my city.
Enter—and central amongst the inmost ring
of brave turrets, you'll find a tower rising
above an open courtyard like a tree
amidst a field of corn. And if its grey
visage looks down on you with sullen aspect
do not blame the old one. For within, there shines
a treasure, the likes of which most men find
only in dream. It is my sister, who,
more beautiful than the stars of deepest night,
anticipates the splendor our castle and our city
offers with bounteous hands.

Gawain:

To what do I owe such blessing, noble sir?
You speak of your sister as of a miracle,
and such are best received without question.
Yet, if I hear aright, you send this stranger
unaccompanied to your sister's side.

Vergulacht:

Yes, unaccompanied, and nameless. A knight
indeed, will go with you, and announce
you as my guest; myself, at first excuse.
I have a most hard task still to perform,
and cannot return before evening comes.
Yet I know, you'll not miss my presence much;
my sister's will cut time quite short enough.
Only—hold to it, that we are bound
nameless: that our names, we'll first give
when—like flower-blossoms—the fair light
of friendship opens them with warming smiles.
Therefore, ask not after city, country, castle,
nor after my fair sister's most fair name.
Forgive me— I must to my work. Follow
this knight; he will be your guide and herald.

(*departs, signing farewell*)

Gawain:

Shall I obey this stranger's call, or hold
more strictly to my search for you, o friend?
An indescribable name sways before me
and cleaves my heart like a spear. It is yours,
Parzival—"midmost through!" Very well.
Not sideways, Gawain! Whatever door
opens before you—enter!

Lead on, Knight! Iwanet, we ride!

Scene 2 In Antikonie's Tower

It is very richly furnished. Tapestries on the walls. In the background, through an open archway, one comes out onto the balcony that encircles the tower. Gawain and Antikonie sit upon a couch. At their feet, a carpet that represents a knightly lady who holds a unicorn in her lap. On a table in front of them, a bowl with grapes and a plate with cakes.

Antikonie:

What you, sir, as one who's nameless, ask
finds answer through another who's without name.
And would it then be strange, if that answer
must bear witness to what is forever nameless?
If I love you? Do you ask in sport?
You came to me as from the golden glow
of heaven, the gentle dawn that spreads before
the rising of the sun. All but the lark
were silent. How presciently did my heart then beat
against its cage! You ask in sport, for sporting
like a falcon on strong, light wings, you flew here.
O sir, remember, that in a woman's heart
every jest turns fast to earnest thought,
and beneath the light blue mirror of the lake,
which laughingly reflects the image of the shore,
the stone of your question quickly sinks to darkness
in its depths.

Gawain:

What in earnest is, what sport—
who can tell this, friend? As at dusk
fair day will disappear into the deep blue scope
of evening, so will light play often plunge
into soft seriousness—the cheerful
beatings of our hearts be weighed down
by sudden sweetness, our soundless breath
wrung by a sigh.

Antikonie:

O friend!

Gawain:

I knew nothing
of you, fair one, when, in dimmest dawn
I mounted my steed, and set out for distant lands.
No singer, playing tenderly upon his harp,
bathed my soul in the wonder of your beauty.
Galloping here, the lightening clouds did break
and from the glowing radiance stepped forth—yourself.

Antikonie:

Do you describe, what I myself have known?
I know not who you are, yet know you well,
for none do I know better than the stranger.

Gawain:

How marvelous, too, your brother's counsel!
This city's name? It is the city of cities!
And this castle's? It is the type of its kind!
And you, beloved, if you bear a name,
it is the name which is in everything,
which—so near and new and inexpressible,
so common and so singular, eternal is—
You! sweetest You! And can You do aught
but return the love of another, loving You?
Say, can it?

Antikonie:

Ah, my friend, the little word you'd fain
tear from my lips, is most like the sharp-edged sword;

burying itself within the heart, it tears
in two the veil of most precious mysteries
and then—? See this bowl here.
Of these two grapes, choose one.

Gawain:
I choose—the red.

Antikonie:
And why just this?

Gawain:
Because it turns to blood. Because glowing
in the blood, love, like wine, is transfigured.

Antikonie:
Take a berry. Wait, consider it
a moment more. I, too, will take one. (*takes a blue grape*)
Contemplate this pure, well-formed round—
a sphere, like the sun, perfect on each
and every side. And yet, it is no sun.
With dense, dark force, Earth enters in
to this small wonder, steeping it in deep,
earnest blue, wherein there dwells humility,
that can do nought else but bend upon the vine,
chastely awaiting what cometh timely to it.
And over all, look, the delicate scent,
the exhalation of a silver breath,
the veil, that wraps and hides sweet mystery.
Is our heart, a woman's love, not thus?
Touch it, and you tear the fair round;
the fine scent vanishes; the gaping wound, bleeds.

Gawain:
And should the berries then hang, until the frost
murders them? Until the black raven
robs the too-ripe booty for a meager meal?
Have you not offered them for our repast?
For what we eat, we indeed do kill, and yet
draw on to new and greater life within
our hearts. Allow me!
(*He eats the berry and jumps up.*)

Antikonie (*likewise rising*):
My friend!

Gawain:
Beloved!

Antikonie:
O, you kill me
and I would die.

Gawain (*embraces her*):
Dark, sweet death! (*He kisses her.*)

(*Teudares rushes in.*)

Teudares:
I'm not mistaken! It's he, the heartless blasphemer,
who killed our king in a distant swamp.
the brazen Gawain!

Antikonie:
Gawain?

Gawain:
What? This castle's named—Shanphanzun?

Teudares:
As surely as you're a cur, lecherous dog!

Gawain:
My sword! Where is it?

Antikonie:
God! Good God!

Teudares:
Don't cry for your sword. You'll not find it,
but only curses, and sharp-toothed revenge.

Gawain:
Liar, what do you accuse me of? You
have never seen my face.

Teudares:

Indeed I have
in the distant land of Bertane, where I
once rode in company with our king; he sought
Arthur there, at the proud and noble court.
One evening I, unthinking, let our King
ride alone into a neighboring wood. He
did not return, yet instead of his, I saw
a hanging head, pale with madded eyes
—yours, o wretch—hunting through the forest;
and soon after, the king, slain in a stinking swamp.
Curse you! Now look upon your death!
(*raises his sword against Gawain*)

Antikonie:

Stop!
Strike this breast, before you strike him down.

Teudares:

What, you shield the killer of my master;
your father's murderer? O, you whore!

Gawain (*he has lifted up a chair*):

Slanderer! Take your reward!
(*smashes the chair against Teudares' head. Teudares' sword falls from him.*)

Teudares (*stumbling out through the open door*):

Ai! Treason!
Over here, all with weapons! To the tower!
Here is the king's murderer! Make haste!
Surround the tower, ring the bells! Storm
over Shanphanzun! Death to the murderer!

Gawain (*throws the door closed after Teudares, and bolts it*) :

Cry, you shameful cock, 'til your throat bursts.
This time you'll not find me entirely unarmed.
(*picks up the sword*)
This will turn against you.

Antikonie (*trembling*):

Are you Gawain?

Gawain:

I am he. In the light of the sun
I'll freely confess my name to one and all.
And never have I raised this arm to perform
a coward's work under the cover of darkness.
Of your father's death, I know nothing;
I swear it by the heavens, and by the force
of Love that, like a lance of holy fire,
tore us into each other's arms.

Antikonie:

You are no murderer;
you cannot be one.

Gawain:

On the strength of Galogandres' word,
offering me safe passage, I rode here
to do grave battle with him, one on one.
Now, it's not Galogandres who falls upon me;
already, all Shanphanzun runs furiously together.
Do you hear the bells? See you there
the hundreds of horsemen coming? Laborers
with staffs and axes already rush together
in answer to that liar's cry for aid.
We are besieged, friend. Now arms decide.
Yet, we'll celebrate our love's festival
so long as we draw breath. And if, perchance,
we succumb to greater force, then, beloved,
we'll breathe out our souls, falling side
by side. Say, shall it be thus?

Antikonie:

Yes.

Gawain:

In greeting, then
and in farewell—to my heart!

(*They embrace.*)

And now, to work.
Do you have no armor in this tower?

Antikonie:

Not a pin.

Gawain:

If I had but a shield!
And if there's none, any kind of board.

Antikonie:

The chessboard.

Gawain:

Perfect! Broad as a door
it covers my body down to the knee.
Black and white, the squares! Life or Death.
Let us see, whether it be white or black
that wins the game. But straps for my arm?

Antikonie:

Take my belt!

Gawain:

And nails?

Antikonie:

Here, in this chest.

Gawain:

Good!
(*He fastens the belt as an armband and handhold on the board.*)
The shield's ready. I am fully armed
for battle. But you, fellow warrior?

Antikonie (*pointing to the chesspieces*):

Here—these are my weapons: pawns, knights,
mighty rooks, and bishops—the great weight
of the King himself must serve me in battle—
and if all else fails, at last—the Queen.

Gawain:

How they rage there! But what will you do
with the toy soldiers?

Antikonie:

Hurl them down.
Does one not do thus when enemies storm walls?

Gawain:

Ha, you are brave!

Antikonie:

Should then Gawain
be shamed by the heart he drew to him?
Well then!

(*She snatches up a big, heavy piece.*)

Gawain:

The door cracks. They're at it with their axes.
Very well, I am ready. Let them come!
The first that storms in, will feel the wrath
of this sword.

Antikonie:

Love is death. The choice is not ours.
Until we meet once more, where Angels dwell.

(*Roaring and cracking at the door, cries from without. Antikonie has stepped onto the balcony; one sees her hurl the the stone pieces down below.*)

Scene 3 In the Courtyard of Shanphanzun

In the middle of the scene, one sees Antikonie's tower. The door of the tower has been splintered by axe-blows, and is broken in. In the doorway, Gawain stands with shield and sword.A mass of farmers, pages, and other sorts—all led by Teudares—fill out the scene. A few wounded ones are born away. The attackers keep a certain safe distance from the door.

Teudares:

You cowards! Heroes only with your tongues.
For three hours you've stormed this tower, and won
only wounds. And yet once more—attack!
Don't you see, how his strength is failing?
Storm the door—and—in!

Farmer 1:

You go first!

Farmer 2:

Why do you set us on him, like dogs, while you stand idle?

Farmer 1:

You're the one who fights
with your mouth.

Others:

Yes, you're the one.

Farmer 1:

Go in and fetch some blows like these.

Farmer 2:

The knight's afire, and if it's not the Devil
that fights for him, then the Lord of Heaven
stands by his side.

Farmer 3:

He fights like a lion.

Teudares:

Storm the door, I say. Shame to those
who'll not do it for the King's honor!

Farmer 1:

That means you.

Teudares:

You rogue! Dare to speak
another word..

Farmer 1:

Not just one—a hundred!
What does this business have to do with us?
Antikonie herself protects the stranger.

Teudares:

She's lost her senses. And you are as she
if you do not obey my word. Attack!
Storm the door!

Farmer 1:

Lead! Lead on! The knight
has precedence.

Teudares (*throwing him towards the door*):

In there, you!

Several:

Stop!
You yourself lead us against him,
or we'll lead you.

Teudares:

You dare. . .

Farmer 2:

Strike! Knock him
to the ground. And over his body, we'll attack.

All:

Down with him!

Farmer 2:

He always despised us, and often
slandered us before the King. Today, he pays!

Another:

When one of us owed, he set the dogs on us,
and when he could, struck us with the whip!

Many:

Pay him back!

Teudares:

Scoundrels! Back! I'll skewer
the first who touches me!

Several:

Strike him.

Others:

Down!

Teudares (*crying out*):
Ah! (*He falls.*)

One:
Break the dog's neck!

(*A hubbub and screams as the mob tramples Teudares. He's dragged to the side*).

Several:
Now, to the tower!

Others:
To the tower!

All:
Storm the door! Attack!

(*General assault upon the tower. Gawain, with his last strength, fends off the attackers. Antikonie appears on the balcony and hurls everything in her room down upon the mob. General outcry.*)

Galogandres (*enters, armed*) :
What's this? What's enraged them? Ha, Gawain
in this tower? And there, on the balcony,
Antikonie, raging like a Greek Goddess!
Stop, I say, stop! Your weapons, down! Do you
not hear the voice of your Count? Give way!
Back from this tower! Who does not wish
to make acquaintance with my sword, stand off!
Here stand I, Galogandres! This knight
came here, assured safe escort by my oath.
Would you dishonor me? Your weapons—down!
(*uproar subsides*)
Gawain is mine. He was challenged by this,
my sword, and soon he'll feel its keen edge
repay him for his crime. ''Til that time,
none has power or right to strike him down.
'Til then, I'll cover him with my sword
as if he were my friend, or my own brother.
Who led you on against him?

Farmer 1 (*pointing to Teudares*) :
That one, there!

Galogandres:
What, Teudares? Who struck him down? Bring him here!
Lay him upon his shield. (*It is done.*)

Woe, death already
shows in his features. Silence!
What is it, Knight? You'd speak? Tell,
for God's sake; tell, what has passed.

Teudares (*weakly*):
Send them away.

Galogandres:
Fall back from here, far off!
Delay not; death comes fast. Already the sweat
breaks upon your brow.

Teudares:
I cannot.

Galogandres:
In a moment, one will question you, whom
you cannot refuse to answer. For the sake
of your soul, and its salvation, speak!

Teudares:
A shade rises up before me, o unspeakable
horror!

Galogandres:
Do not turn away, Teudares,
look me in the eye!

Teudares:
Woe to me!

Galogandres:
Speak, speak!

Teudares:

I killed the King.

Galogandres:

You? O God!
You speak madness; it cannot be.

Teudares:

He denied me Antikonie—

Galogandres:

Revenge—?

Teudares:

I threw the dead one in the swamp;
his yellow face looked horribly up at me—
(*with wide staring eyes*)
The King! Help! Save me! (*He dies*).

Galogandres:

Your salvation
lies no more with men. His eyes roll—
Cover him! Bear him away. All, gather round!
I have something to tell you, that will make
your blood run cold. Hear, what I say, in silence!

Voices:

The King!

(*All give way, Vergulacht with dirtied, bloodflecked armor steps, pale and with bowed head, into the circle.*)

Vergulacht:

Who's born away there? Why the weapons?
Why all gathered round, as if expecting. . . ?

Galogandres:

The murderer of your father is discovered.

Vergulacht:

What, not Gawain?

Galogandres:

Death's confession
weighs heavier than living lie.
Teudares killed the King.

Vergulacht:

What, his truest,
his best servant? How am I to comprehend. . .

Galogandres:

He desired Antikonie for his wife,
—you know it, sir—and was denied.
That drove him to revenge.

Vergulacht:

Sacrilege!

Galogandres:

But in this fray, the murder has been avenged;
Teudares himself struck down. As for Gawain—
he's innocent. So from his prison, you yourself
may free him.

Vergulacht:

What? Gawain imprisoned?

Galogandres:

In the tower. Teudares rallied the people
to besiege him there. With naked sword,
he still stands beneath the broken door.

Vergulacht:

Gawain?

Galogandres:

None other, truly.

Vergulacht:

He whom I invited as guest, is Gawain?
The noble one was so shamefully welcomed?
Make way—I hasten to return him to his freedom.
(*approaches the tower*)

My dear friend, pardon, what happened here.
It was not my will; as I myself
was engaged in hard and bitter battle,
a villain hath betrayed both you and me,
the same, who once accused you of murder.
He is gone. The deed that he has done
has now gripped him; the pale fist he raised
seized its author, and hurled him to damnation.
Sheath your sword; step forth from the cloister
and give me your knightly hand in affirmed friendship.

Gawain:

This is the sword, that performed the deed.
I cast it from me! Yet before I greet you,
let me first lead brave Antikonie
out of this tower. If destiny had not turned,
she would have lain here slain, alongside me.

Vergulacht:

Antikonie! Beloved sister! Bring her to me!

Antikonie (*hurrying into Vergulacht's arms*) :

My brother!

Vergulacht:

O Antikonie, your life
was almost lost, as in a game! What fury
in fate! Your hair's all atangle.

Antikonie:

But brother,
your face is ashen; blood flecks your armor.
What has happened?

Vergulacht:

A knight wished to pass through my choicest pasture;
a serf of mine barred his way; the hot knight
threw him down. I challenged him... we rode...
and I return—fallen, and defeated.

Antikonie:

Who was the knight?

Vergulacht:

A mighty one, surely.
I do not know his name, though never has
a mortal fought with such enormous force.
At first he stood, unmoving—let my lance
break against him, and my sword-blows rain
like hail on his head while he stared, brooding,
into darkest night. Then suddenly,
he towered up, and a fiery glow burst
like lightning from blows no man could withstand.

Gawain:

His armor—what color?

Vergulacht:

Red, like fire—
no, red like blood.

Gawain:

It is he. The knight can be none other.
Where did you fight him?

Vergulacht:

In the wood,
where we first met.

Gawain:

O, what mischance!
So close—and yet, passed by.

Vergulacht:

Tell me his name!

Gawain:

It is Parzival.

All:

Ha, Parzival!

Gawain:

A name that sounds above all other men's
like a bell above the clash of battle.

I must to him. At this very moment,
I must leave you.

Antikonie:
Gawain!

Gawain:
Just as a knife
suddenly scissors the most splendid weaving,
so does this name quickly cut in two
all ties that hold me. King, you've lost
no honor in this battle. But tell me, how
must you pay the penalty of your defeat?

Vergulacht:
From this day on, I must ride for a year
in search of the Grail.

Gawain:
O Parzival!

Vergulacht:
Your eyes brim with tears! What does this mean?

Gawain:
So the yearning for the light of the Grail
breaks into flame within you, illumining
once more the grim hollow in your breast.
King, let the promise that you gave him
pass over to me; I will fulfill it, will,
this very hour, ride out in search of the Grail,
even if this may seem a foolish—nay—
an impossible task. So give me leave, then,
all of you, to go. . . . Bring me my page
and let us bid farewell.

Vergulacht:
If you must,
then I shall not hinder you. My love
goes with you.

Galogandres:

Forgive, O hero. I challenged you
because I thought you guilty.

Gawain:

Be my friend.

Galogandres:

And you mine!

Gawain (*to Antikonie*):

Precious one,
you look at me with moist and vacant eyes.

Antikonie:

My brother, Galogandres, all of you—
grant me a moment with him, alone.

Vergulacht:

You'll not ask in vain. Let us part.
(*embraces Gawain, and departs with the others*)

Antikonie:

I was ready to die with you. Will you
now leave me? Will you go from me as quickly
as you came?

Gawain:

Does the star that sinks
on heaven's horizon, dearest, leave your eye?
Does it not rise new, again and again,
inside you? Say, in truth, is not all parting
mere appearance? I leave you? Spill
the holy draught of beauty, and of Love?
No, I remain close as a brother to you
wherever I go, wherever fate bears you—
you white swan—forward on its darkling waves.

Antikonie:

Let me go with you!

Gawain:

Not even so, beloved. Antikonie, you star,
be who you are. Do not leave your orbit;
revolve still around the circle appointed you
by the creator, illumining all with your light grace.
For we are eternal only within ourselves.
And so—live well.

Antikonie:

If you go, you leave death
behind in me.

Gawain:

Then let death be. There is
no life without death.

Antikonie:

O, would that I could die
upon your breast!

(*They embrace.*)

Gawain:

Live well.

Antikonie:

Live well. Love knows no end.

(*She leaves, passing Iwanet, who arrives with riding gear.*)

Act III Orgeluse

The action takes place in front of the Castle Logrois and upon a lawn near the castle.

Scene 1

A lady with a wounded knight in her lap; behind them, in another space, Orgeluse, combing her hair before a mirror, and singing.

Orgeluse:

Despised be the day in its glitter
praised be the night!
Praised be the secret one, the deep one
the sweet one; praised
be the night!
She removes the veil from off the face
so it breathes, at last, in clarity.
O secret source of revelation,
O sweet, smiling, star-strewn night:
O well of the heavens that is
without beginning
and is beautiful.

Lady:

Be still, you siren! Should your bewitched lullaby
poison even his departing moments?
His blood streams inward, oppressing the heart
you stole from me, you thief! Yes, so wholly
did you tear him from me, that he, dumbstruck,
dragged himself here just so he might die
at your feet. O, when he's gone, you she-devil—
from then on—my one prayer will be a curse
like to a river that ne'er runs dry, a chain
that will not break, "til the end of the world.

Orgeluse (*continuing as before, as if unhearing*) :

Well of the heavens,
sweet Night.
What do you send me?

Is it only silver? Is it gold? Is it diamond-shine?
The cradle of all things is crystal.
There, Truth will be revealed.
Eia, Truth! Eia, the Truth!

Lady:

Beloved, do not hear her; hear me, hear my voice. . . .

(*Gawain and Iwanet, on horses, appear in the foreground.*)

Iwanet:

No further, sir!

Gawain:

How so, child?

Iwanet:

We stray ever further from his trail.

Gawain:

His trail? Did we not lose all sign of him
years ago? He has vanished into nothingness
as he promised. I fear we'll not reach him.

Iwanet:

O sir, I beg you, do not lose hope, for all
is lost with her. Ask not: will I find him?
Rather say: I must.

Gawain:

Must? How, if Heaven
does not will it? Have we not bravely searched
the encircling lands, probed dark forests
where there was neither path, nor guiding star
to light our way, climbed mountains that had never known
a horse's hoof? And wherever we went
was our question not always for him, and for
the Grail? And yet found—neither.

Iwanet:

Still, sir, please,
go no further here.

Gawain:

To turn back
was never my way. And he, for whom we search—
will he ever turn round? Believe me, child,
if we are ever to reach him, it will be
by pressing onward; no other means will do.

Iwanet:

The shield, there, look—it is hacked to pieces.

Gawain:

What's happened here?

(*Gawain and Iwanet dismount and approach a lady. partially hidden behind a bush, a wounded knight unconscious in her lap*)

Lady:

O noble sir, look!

Gawain:

Allow me. (*He examines the wounded knight.*)

He lives yet. His wounds, I think,
need not be fatal, but the blood-flow's dammed
and clots the heart. Be so good, mistress,
as to bend the green bough down to me.
Your knife, Iwanet! I'll peel the bark
and make a straw. Now place it in the wound,
lady, and draw the stopped blood... Look, look,
already his eyes open!

Lady:

Beloved!

Urians (*with weak voice*):

Ah, I live! Life
appeared to me as a thing light as a cloud,
a lovely, white dawning....
Who is the Knight?

Lady:

You owe to him this breath
of life.

Urians:

Ah, I thank you, my friend, and helper.
You came just in time. But tell me, what
leads you here? O, take my counsel, leap quick
upon your horse, and fly this hellish place.
The castle on the mountain, the shimmering
terraces, the garden full of enchanting flowers: all
this splendor is nought but lie. And if you see,
but once, the countess of the castle, her dark eyes
shining like the night, your shaken heart
is wholly lost; you'll storm from there
to fight for her, not knowing that no man
can win the contest, for here the mortal battle
is tried with more than weapons.

Iwanet:

O sir, I beg of you, go no further!

Gawain:

Silence, child! Speak further, knight; tell,
if you have strength, what befell you there.

Urians:

Know, then, of him who cast me to my shame:
Lischoys Gewelljus. He is no hero, believe me,
made of manly force, rather Hell itself
serves him, and each blow you strike will merely
magnify his strength. Go, ride, flee
as quickly as you came!

Gawain:

I am a knight,
and would sooner die, than flee. Where
is Gewelljus? I'll challenge him, without delay.

Urians:

Do you see that shield?

Gawain:

And if mine, too,
were hacked to splinters—should that concern me?

Urians:

You'll not hear me?

Gawain:

I am a fish,
that cannot swim backwards.

Urians:

It is a matter of life and death.

Gawain:

So let it be.

Urians:

Then ride and lose
all you are. Yet if, perchance, you gain
the victory, be so kind as to return here—
I'll not live much longer—and protect this lady!

Gawain:

That will I do, and, meanwhile, my page
will stay with you.

Iwanet:

Sir, I beg you—!

Gawain:

Enough! No one
can prevent my going. You'll see me again.
See to him, Lady. Live well! (*Gawain exits.*)

Iwanet:

Alas! He betrays the goal we both pursue—
betrays himself!

Scene 2

Gawain encounters Orgeluse.

Gawain (*stock-still, as if frozen*):
What a face! What features! Have I e'er,
"til now, known beauty?

Orgeluse (*looks up*):
Who speaks?

Gawain:
O you star
of deepest night, you sun of all seas,
you splendor of the heart, look not away
so we might gaze thus, eye in eye, eternally.

Orgeluse:
What a palaverer, a man who plays with words
as if with fencing foils! But is't not said, that he
who cannot act, relies the more on prattle?

Gawain:
The words, which I now do speak, are your own!
You place them in my heart, and in my spirit,
you fount of all beauty. To look on you
is eternity. Who are you? Did you descend
from a throne of white cloud? Or did the sea
birth you from out its green womb, and bear you
over its glassy waves on delicate foam
as if on shimmering flower-blossoms?

Orgeluse:
Your stuttering, mine? Your word-bungling?
I see, sir, that you are hardly modest.
And stop gawking at me so, or I'll soon think
I was put here on display for the pleasure
of every vain, ill-mannered coxcomb.

Gawain:
You are not, as you speak.

Orgeluse:

What?

Gawain:

You are,
what I alone know—without doubt
are hidden from yourself. For if you knew
your being, you would not disgrace it thus.

Orgeluse:

Disgrace? What language! No sooner allow
this tongue-twister a bit of conversation
than he falls into brazen impudence.
I have wasted enough time on you already.
If you're courteous enough to heed my word—
then go, leave my sight, and quickly too.

Gawain:

What a riddle, O wondrous friend,
you are to me. You fume, you chide me hence,
yet I cannot obey the sentence of your speech,
for as I list your beauteous lips, the sense
of your words is secretly transfigured;
it is as if I hear a tender praising,
a soft beseeching that, for all eternity
I should never leave you—

Orgeluse:

Have you gone wholly
out of your mind? To put your own vain wish
in place of what I myself clearly pronounced,
exchanging reality for fond delusion!
Go, I tell you!

Gawain:

Pardon, I'll not go.
I know you. You called me here, and when
I saw you, my heart began to quiver—yea,
shuddered in recognition. Do not turn
your face from me; here is the soul's mirror.
I know my truth. You'll give me Love, or break
your own heart.

Orgeluse:

Love? You require
what no one can demand, what was, and is,
and ever will be, the free offer of the heart?
Command the sun to shine on you, and she
—the moment you have spoken—angrily hides
her glorious countenance in a veil of dark cloud.

Gawain:

I say once more: it is your words that speak,
your own lips that issue my commands.
Look not in the glass, look at me,
and I will tell you how endlessly radiant
the beauty is that God poured forth in you.
And if I stutter, can you scold me then for that?
For is not my stuttering more eloquent
than all the silver-tongued songs of poets?
Do not scorn yourself. You cannot turn
your heart from me—

Orgeluse:

You donkey, I tell you
I can do what I will, and could hurl you
so deep in the pit of your foolishness
that neither sun nor moon would shine on you.
I could also engage you in my service.
Yet woe to you, vain idler, if I do!

Gawain:

So speak the word; hang on me the woe
you threaten. For with this woe
I will fill myself; it shall be heaven,
light, and everything to me. Will you accept me?

Orgeluse:

Yes, you fool, and ride with you straightaway.
I'll send you forth to battle against another
and will not rest, until you lie, howling,
and breathe out your life like a beast in the wood.

Gawain:

I am your knight.

Orgeluse:

Do you men then believe
the flower-blossom unfolds its beauty just so
you may pluck it with your brazen hands?
Is woman, then, to you, but an object
of desire, a kind of booty, stalked like a hind
so that your coward-spear might pierce it through?
You are the masters of our bodies—how is that?
We're cast beneath you, like a piece of bait
for the eagle, circling the air for the kill?
We are surrendered, helpless, to your will?
No, noble hero, you who have left so many
maidens in pain and shame, do not imagine
that your deeds will never turn against you.
For I—know it—am the vengeance of my sex,
which your wickedness shames each day and hour.
You have chosen her, so drink the cup
she offers you!

Gawain:

I will drink it, mistress,
drain it to the dregs—call me a fool
if that bitter bottom does not shimmer with gold.
(*approaches her*)

Orgeluse:

Don't touch me. Bring me my palfrey
from the garden so we may ride forth.
With this, you may hold the reins of my horse.

(*Orgeluse draws out two white gloves. She gives one to Gawain, and pulls the other on, takes and holds the reins of Gawain's horse in her gloved hand, so he may go after hers.*)

Do not tarry!

Orgeluse (*singing*):

*Disdained be the Day in its Glitter
Praised be the Night!
Praised be the secret one, the deep one,
the sweet one,
praised be the Night!*

Gawain (*returns to Orgeluse*):

Here is your palfrey. Should I, mistress, now
lift you into the saddle?

Orgeluse:

Do not dare!
Did I not say, I'll scorn you like the plague!
And like the plague, will persecute you—such
will be the thanks for your so noble service.
Before this day is done, I will see you
hacked to pieces like a thistle in a hail-storm.
Your horse!
(*She throws the glove she has pulled off her hand.*)

Gawain:
(*picks up the glove and stuffs it in his breast with the other glove*)

Lady, I carry both of your beloved hands
upon my heart, and so fear neither shame
nor death.

Scene 3

The setting is similar to Scene 1; Gawain and Orgeluse have met Iwanet a short way off from Urians and his Lady.

Iwanet (*grasping Gawain's reins as if to stop him*):

Sir, this may not be, you mustn't
ride with that false one!

Gawain:

You too? Hold your tongue, and mount up, quickly—
you follow me as the page of this, our lady.

Iwanet:

And our goal?

Gawain:

I told you, my way to him
leads through the midst of things themselves.

Iwanet:

You are lost,
lost in the spell of this enchantress,
and have forgotten him, whom we seek!

Gawain:

Quiet!

Iwanet:

I will not be quiet, Sir—I may not.
We must leave this place!

Gawain:

Will you anger me
yet more? Mount up, and come!

Iwanet:

I'll not do it.

Gawain:

What?

Iwanet:

If you betray him,
I—will betray you!

Gawain:

You'll deny me service?

Iwanet:

O let me beg of you. . . .

Gawain:

Not a word
more of that, boy!

Iwanet:

If you so insist,
then I am released —
(*mounts his horse*)

Gawain:

Boy, are you mad?

Iwanet:
I know, to whom I go—

Gawain:
You will—?

Iwanet:
Live well!
I will never, never see you again. (*springs away*)

Orgeluse (*laughing out loud*):
A fine boy! Does he not model his master
to a T?

Gawain:
Farewell!

Orgeluse:
Soon, I'll call
the same after you. So come then, make haste
to lose your life and honor.

Gawain:
Lady, wait
a moment more. I see a rare herb
that will heal the knight's bleeding wound.
Let me pluck it!

Orgeluse:
Better let him die!
And you, who understand the art of herbs
as well as speech, from henceforth, I will call
Quack-Quack. The name suits you well—
you, who minister so tenderly to villains.

Gawain (*who has dismounted and brought the herb to Urians*):
I'll place this on your wound, dear brother.
Breathe deeply! And you, lady, draw gently!
As soon as the herb's juice mixes with his blood,
new life and power will course quickly through him.

Urians:

Ah, that is better. Can it be that I
am well? Help me up. O, the joy
of life! Ha, I am free! Could I not even
stay the saddle? Since you have done me one
good turn, my friend, you'll not stint a second.
Lend me your horse, so I might ride a bit
and test my new-found strength.

Gawain:

If the lady
so consents— her wish alone decides.

Orgeluse:

Give him the horse, if your honor, Quack-Quack,
is so inclined. He'll break his neck the faster.

Gawain:

So take it.

Urians (*mounts the horse*) :

Lady, quick, follow my example,
mount your horse, so we might, for our pleasure,
take a turn around the fields. For look—
the wonder of the herb is such that I
feel stronger than before.

Lady (*has mounted her horse*):

Eh, how bold
you look about! What is it that you think of?

Urians:

I'll tell you. Now I am mounted, I may
discover to this proud knight the name I bear.
He is Gawain— I know him all too well—
the world holds him to be a noble hero
though truly, I know, the case is quite otherwise.
For I am Urians! —Know it, Gawain! —
and sit upon your proud and noble horse.
Since I've lost mine in battle, and because
it so pleases me, I think I'll keep it ever.

Gawain:

You—Urians? Woe, give me back my horse!
Did I bring you back to life, so you
might treat me thus?

Urians:

O most worthy one,
you, guardian of innocence, who thinks
that you must free the dove from the vulture's
bloody clasp—what concern of yours is it
if I take a maid? And if it's a child?
You cleric! Doesn't every young girl yearn
for the one who tears her little garland?
Virginity—that is a delicate drink
that spoils in the sun.

Gawain:

Maiden-robber! Rogue!

Urians:

The maidens all thank you here through the mouth
of Urians, who serves them better than hypocrites
who hide their lewd intent behind the mask
of self-righteous piety. Now,
live well and may the purity of your heart
wing your feet. Come, my dear one.

(*Urians prepares to ride away; Orgeluse laughs brightly.*)

Gawain:

My horse! Must I from now on go on foot?

Urians (*from some distance*):

Gawain, look, I am thankful for the help
you gave me. See there— here comes a noble rider
with a winged steed. Win it from him,
and you will have swift substitute for your own.

Lady:

My friend, you should not behave so!

Urians:

Not so? Do I only appear to be your lover?
Do I lie with you only to count the stars?
The hypocrite! Come! *(exits with the Lady)*

(*Malcreature trots out on a wretched nag.*)

Gawain:

Who is the monster?

Orgeluse:

Our page, knight—
at your service for this—"ride"— for he
resembles you, like one eye, the other.

Gawain:

I have no choice; I must win his horse.
Permit me.

Orgeluse:

To your special honor—
and if the rib-thin beast can carry you,
you can thank heaven for its generous blessing.

Gawain (*confronting Malcreature*):

Halt, fellow!

Malcreature (*shrieking*):

Shame! Shame on you!
You'd be so brazen as to lead the proud countess
about with you? O, your stupid side
put that idea in your head. What, do you think
the rose blooms for you alone? Your dumb hands
reach out for it and—O fool!—they grasp the thorn!
Beauty's but a snare for hasty palms—
Curse you, you rash, proud, thoughtless . . .

Gawain (*throwing him from his horse*):

Will you be quiet, foul-mouth?

Malcreature (*with loud howling*):

Auh! O woe! O woe!
May the devil tear the flesh from your bones!

Gawain:

Curses fly like arrows back to those
who send them. (*contemplates the horse*)
So these skin and bones are supposed to carry me?

Orgeluse:

Doesn't it suit you?
Why hesitate to mount your brave racehorse?
On him, you'll no doubt win the battle. Now
gaze into this mirror, knight—what you see
reflected there, is your very self:
a proud, well-mounted hero, specially
elected to possess the fairest beauty.
And yet— before the fact— she's not yet his.
And since the mistress feels no great urge
to ride beside such splendor— the less so since
at any moment, it may collapse— she'll ride
ahead to the river, and there, where it roars
out of the deep woods, she— true and constant
as she is— will await you, expectantly,
by the field of battle. Fare you well! (*rides off*)

Malcreature (*limping off*):

Farewell, with all the devil's blessings!

Scene 4

A small field by the river; towards the background, the field widens to a broad plain. The river is dark and wide and splendid in its flow. On the far shore are great ash trees. The Ferryman's house, with boats, is visible in a cove. Immediately behind the forest, upon a mount enchantingly covered with trees and gardens, is the Castle of Marvels. All the windows of the fort, all the balconies and turrets, are occupied by beautifully clothed women who look down upon the broad plain.

Orgeluse (*on her horse by the river*):

Hey, ferryman, ferryman, make haste, row over!

Ferryman (*from the far shore*):

Who calls?

Orgeluse:

The duchess.

Ferryman:

I come. (*unties his boat*)

Orgeluse:

I see Lischoys
Gewelljus disporting himself on the battlefield.
Good, he keeps watch, just as I had hoped.
Though truly, he has little cause to celebrate
for no sooner has he thrown one man in the grass
than I lead another proud one to him,
so he may break his bones as well.
O men, you fools, so loyal in your service
that I readily ruin one through the other!
For each who fancies himself a conqueror,
I find a stronger— and so drive each one
into the maw of shame and death, and yet still
all are willing to perform the gruesome service.
And when they kneel before me with upraised arms
should I not seem to myself to be— a goddess?
And yet, how sad, to sit upon the throne
which they, in boorishness, have built me,
showering scorn, instead of grace, upon them
and so be nought but the idol of rutting fools.
O what pain and shame then fills me
in the night, when men lay down their arms,
and awakened fountains murmur mysteries
no blind day will e'er unseal for me!

Ferryman:

Here I am.

Orgeluse:

Tie the boat on the shore. Remain here!
And when I give the word, row me across
the flowing current.

Ferryman:

As you command.

Orgeluse:

Shortly, there will be another battle.
There comes the knight, now.

Ferryman:

A young hero, and handsome,
too. But his nag—! By God, it is the mare
of Malcreature!

Orgeluse:

It is. And its rider, too
will bear the name the beast so fitly carries,
as soon as he springs upon its back: Malcreature!

Ferryman:

Is this not the name of all people, Lady?

Orgeluse:

If not all mankind,
at least— all men.

Ferryman:

What, and not women?
Where is the creature, of whom one might say:
she is not only beautiful, but also— good?

Orgeluse:

Are not these two one?

Ferryman:

Amongst angels
they are the same. And yet our kind is made
to veil itself.

Orgeluse:

We are vales, yes.
In dark vales, souls hide their greatest wonder,
greater far than the splendor of the castle
on that high hill. Do you recognize it?

Ferryman:

Quiet now. Those who know, keep silent.

(*Gawain arrives, leading the horse behind him.*)

Orgeluse:

Welcome, hasty hero! I have today
chid you unjustly, now I see that wisdom
shines from your brow. How quickly you have grasped
that sometimes one may go faster on foot
than mounted on the saddle of a nag!

Gawain:

Is this the battlefield?

Orgeluse:

Eh? you look about
as if awaiting the hangman.
And indeed, not far off, you'll find
a hero, who will take your breath away.
Mount your warhorse, and ride— to the field!
And yet— before you go, lift your gaze
to the castle-towers, touched already
by the evening sun, and there, through
the vaulted windows, see what seem rising stars—
the eyes of the castle-maidens, raying down
in deepening twilight. If you count them
(which, perchance, you may; one often finds
such culture in a knight) you'll find four hundred
that shall bear fair witness to your fall.
Have you made your peace with this world?
Then look— drink of that heavenly well,
and go forth, comforted, to your demise.

Gawain:

And you?

Orgeluse (*leading her palfrey to the boat*):

I'll board this boat, and ride over.

Gawain:

Woe, you'll not linger here, while I
do battle for you?

Orgeluse:

Knight, you'll fall and bleed
in the grass, and such a sight, believe me,
I've no wish to see— for I have seen it
too often already.

Gawain:

You flee?

Orgeluse:

I ferry.

Gawain:

I'll not see you again?

Orgeluse:

No.

Gawain:

And if I prevail?

Orgeluse:

Prevail,
and what follows, will find itself.

Gawain:

Then, to it!
(*Gawain mounts the horse; Orgeluse is ferried over the river.*)

Gawain:

Her *nay* is *yea*— I'm not deceived— I'll try it,
were I without so much as spear and shield.
But my horse? He will fall, and crumple
at the first pass. So be it! My foe's steed
will stumble too, and toss him in the grass.
When we leap up— his sword will be no better.
For Orgeluse! No, for you, whom I know
is hid in Orgeluse's husk, and pours beauty
into her proud features! (*rides toward the battlefield*)

Ferryman (*lands, and sings as he makes fast his boat*):

The waving river is meeting
the near and the far shores;
I, too, come in greeting—
then quickly lift my oars.

Neither this side, nor that
offers me rest, or peace,
and so my constant habit
is rowing without cease.

No bridge spans the river
no track crosses o'er;
your vision's light quiver
scarce marks the far shore.

The landsmen, here and there,
all call the weary ferryman
to hurry to their care
and be their endless waterman.

When will the ferryman climb
out of his boat on land?
When distant shores incline
to rest hand in hand?

(*climbs ashore*)

The clashing of swords, the din of battle, ceases.
The fight is done, and silence falls from heaven
as often before events of grave import.
The battle was brief. Upon his feeble steed
the young hero must've fallen at the first pass.
Gewelljus' sword is hard and unforgiving—
it knows only death. . .

(*He turns upstage. Gawain appears, leading his own horse.*)
Gewelljus defeated! The victor, leading Gewelljus' horse!

Gawain:
Tell me, ferryman; the duchess, where has she gone?

Ferryman:
O sir, you'll not see her again this night.
Though now that you've won victory, she
will choose you for her knight— not out of love,
but out of wickedness— sir, I speak the truth.
She'll put you in Gewelljus' place, where you
must mercilessly conquer all who trespass
this enchanted ground. See these flowers—
petals bright and gaudy, but with dark centers
filled with sorrow: the earth in which they grow
is soaked with blood. Do not let yourself
be thus used, O noble knight; tear
off the mortal snares that are winding tight
around your soul! I swear, I give true counsel.

Gawain:
We'll see about that.

Ferryman:
Look me in the face!
Say, do I have reason, to mislead you?

Gawain:
Good, good, ferryman— I trust your grey hair
well enough. It grows dark, so tell me:
where can I spend this night?

Ferryman:
My house stands
upon the far shore. If you like, you
may be my guest; I'll share with you all I have.

Gawain:
Some food, and a bed to sleep in, is all I ask.

Ferryman:
Then come. Guide your horse into the boat.
Evening's arriving. A river of gold
runs along the stream. See that little light?
We steer towards it. Do you know what it means
to cross over the river as night is falling?

Gawain (*guiding his horse into the boat*):

It means, that one wishes to come to the far shore.

Ferryman:

The far shore! Seat yourself, take the helmet
off your head; the night air will cool you.
Is that not pleasant? Good! The current already
grasps and lifts the boat, bearing us away.

ACT IV: Klingsohr

Scene 1 Room in the Ferryman's House

In the background a large curtain, covered with all kinds of rare birds and animals. When it is opened, one can step out onto a balcony, and from there, above the tops of the trees, one can see the Castle of Marvels.

To the side, a bed is made ready. In the foreground, to the right, a cloth-covered table, to which the Ferryman brings food. In the front, to the left, Gawain, and Bene. It is night, the curtain is closed, and candles light the room.

Ferryman:

Look after this knight, my child, as if he were
our own master. I offered him food and shelter;
his gracious presence honors us here tonight.
(*goes in and out preparing the meal*)

Bene (*kneeling before Gawain*):

So accept me as your maid, O master.

Gawain:

Stand up. You need not kneel. I am not God,
nor even a king.

Bene:

Even so, I am here to serve you.

Gawain:

Well, if you would like,
help me shed this cold, unyielding iron.

Bene:

Allow me! (*She begins loosening his armor.*)

Gawain:

You are so solemn, child
as if you were taking the sacrament.

Bene:

O sir,
now I loose the armor from your tired limbs,
and will soon remove your raiment too.
For at night, the world unveils itself,
and man, too, casts off his coverings.

Gawain:

And breathes more deeply.

Bene:

Starlight is the eye of Heaven. At night
the heavens first begin to shimmer, and when
the husks that hide him fall away, Man, too,
shines more brightly.

Gawain:

You marvelous child;
from where does such speech come to you?

Bene:

It is truth, that I speak. I see it always.

Gawain:

The knight dons his armor in the morning
to steel himself for hard, cold conflict;
at evening, the light of triumph shines in him
but at night, he is fed.

Bene:

When first his armor
is off. For clothed in iron, he cannot receive
true nourishment.

Gawain:

O child, is not the speech
you offer, itself food and drink?

Bene:

I serve you, sir, with all I am. If you hunger
eat of me; if you are thirsty—then drink.

Ferryman:

The meal is ready. If it please you, sir,
you may take your place.

Gawain:

Let the child
share the meal with me. The magic of her speech
feeds me more than earthly nourishment.

Ferryman:

Join our guest, child.

Bene:

I do as you desire. (*joins Gawain at the table*)

Ferryman:

May God bless what is here prepared for you. (*exits*)

Gawain:

Will you consecrate the cup with your lips?

Bene:

What you say, I shall do, for you are a knight,
and your word, the pledge of chivalry.
(*She sips from his cup, and then offers it to Gawain.*)

Gawain:

The stars shine in this wine. I feel their breath
upon your lips. What is your name?

Bene:

Bene.

Gawain:

And how old are you, Bene?

Bene:

Twelve years.

Gawain:

Strange. You remind me of another child
kin to me—and yet, recall to my heart

Antikonie as well; and Orgeluse,
too, hovers in the depths of your soul. Alas!

Bene:

You sigh?

Gawain:

Break some bread for me. And take, too,
for yourself.

Bene:

I do as you bid.

Gawain:

And if I bid evil?

Bene:

You cannot wish evil, sir.

Gawain:

O, my child, do not say that. Evil
is inborn within the heart.

Bene:

No, sir,
the heart is God's possession, and God is good.

Bene:

Will you eat no more?

Gawain:

I am no longer hungry, nor do I thirst.

Bene:

The stars feed us with their secret fullness.
Do you wish to rest?

Gawain:

Child—

Bene:

I'll ready your bed.

(*She carries the table off, and turns the bed back.*)

Gawain:

You will serve me as a boy would, too?

Bene:

I am your page, as well.

Gawain:

And your father so consents?

Bene:

He gave me into your noble, knightly hands.

Gawain:

He trusts me so?

Bene:

Yes, sir.

Gawain:

And you?

Bene:

I have surrendered my will to yours.

Gawain:

Then let me rest, for my limbs are weary
from battle.

(*He stretches out.*)

Will you remain by me, Bene?

Bene:

I will make my bed at your feet,
yet will stay awake, until you sleep.

(*She lays a pillow upon the carpet in front of Gawain's bed, and covers herself with her coat.*)

See, I'll lie here.

Gawain:

Reach me your hand
so I might hold it yet a moment more,
and bid you good night. For sleep, I fear,
will shortly overcome me.

Bene:

God bless your rest.

Gawain:

You look wide-awake. Your beautiful eyes
are so full of brightness. How is it, then,
that we lie here, hand in hand?

Bene:

Ah, I'll not think on it, for to me
it is so familiar.

Gawain:

Familiar, you say. How strange!
Do I know you?

Bene:

If you know yourself.

Gawain:

The stars, I think, are kin to us.

Bene:

A ship of silver bears us over the sea.

Gawain:

The waves are music, and a host of spirits
greets us, blowing on fluted conch shells.

Bene:

You smile, and I smile, and the stars
dance freely.

Gawain:

O how fair it is,
how without bound, the waves, the sea, the heavens.

Bene:

Do you know me?

Gawain:

Yes.

Bene:

Do I know you?

Gawain:

Sister, sister.

Bene:

Twelve stars it is, so over, so under
the sea.

Gawain:

Is midnight not near?

Bene:

Already at the threshold.
Do you still hear me?

Gawain:

From far.

Bene:

You flee! You flee!

Gawain:

To you— (*He sleeps.*)

Bene:

To me. The stars go under.
(*Her hand slips out of his; she sleeps.*)

Ferryman:

Bene—! Asleep? Your bed at his feet—
your fair head sunk down upon the pillow.
Innocence smiles in your features. Hero,
you are of the right sort. You've passed
this trial. For the child I entrusted to you
was not to be touched. So now, be blessed!
Let me watch over your holy sleep, you two
pure ones, through this brief, lucent night
so full of mystery. Let song and the sounds
of the harp fill your drifting dreams.

SONG Ferryman's Night-Song:

Night is, upon seven strings my song sounds
the tones of the seven stars.
Night is, my silver song hovers
among the crystal blue heights.

Night is, my boat sails over seven seas
to the distant holy land.
Night is, singing, it moors
upon the shore, the blessed strand.

Night is, the dew of seven heavens
falls into my heart.
Night is, the eternal blue
closes round me, my womb and my grave.

Night is, in the midst of things occurs
the change, the mysterious fall.
Night is, my song fills with coolness
and the stars bend down— all.

Night is, the fair countenance fades,
and the rooster heralds the dawn.
Night is, the wonder is spent
and the boat long turned, and gone.

Day comes, when the stars run to gold,
and the reef springs out of the deeps.
Day comes, when the snow blushes soft;
the ship wrecks on the rocks, and sleeps.

(*As dawn is breaking, the ferryman takes Bene in his arms and carries her out.*)

Scene 2

Gawain (*awakens and sits up*):
The day—! It brings me Orgeluse, as the Night
brought me Orgeluse. And yet the day
offers her as image only, cut off
from my own heart, and wakes the flaming desire

to rend this crude corset, and so to run
out of myself, even as loosed blood streams
out of a mortal wound. O, I rested
by her, in her, embraced and illumined
in the glow of her love, thrilled through and through.
For this I hold to be but foolishness—
that love is single, so one might truly speak
of love, and yet remain forever without answer.
For who does not, and never may, love me
cannot awake the pleasing agony
that so riddles my heart, for a guiding hand
draws the dumb metal of the harp-strings on
to sweet accord—no idle of breath of wind.
But listen, the birds already are awake
and regale the dawn with cheerful chatter.
So welcome day, even if you conceal
what in dream was mine, most inwardly.
Let the balsam of your breath strengthen me
for new deeds!

(*He opens the curtain and notices the Castle of Marvels that lies before him in the early morning light.*)

O, what a sight! The vision that charmed me
at evening rises before me once again;
the fairest castle I have ever beheld
hangs as if suspended in heaven's gold
And look—even before the morning breaks,
and twilight still weaves its shadowy veils
on the threshold twixt night and day,
the castle maidens are awake. They gaze
out from the tower battlements and balconies,
their darklit faces full of dreamy longing,
so beautiful, and yet—like caged birds—
so sorrowful, as if the wondrous castle—
which scarce seems a solid thing of stone—
were not their rightful home. Who will help
unpuzzle the mystery hidden in their deep eyes?

(*Gawain continues in quiet contemplation of the castle.*)

Ferryman:

I wish you good morning, noble sir.

I heard you walking to and fro, and came
to see what service I might perform.

Gawain:

What is that castle called?

Ferryman:

O sir, I bid you
do not ask.

Gawain:

Why not? It shines so close
and clear, as if I might reach out this hand
and touch it. Should I turn away as if
I had never glimpsed the wondrous vision?

Ferryman:

It would indeed be better, if you did.

Gawain:

Yet I have seen it, and cannot forget
the haunting image.

Ferryman:

That is its curse!

Gawain:

Curse? How can such beauty
be accursed?

Ferryman:

Its beauty *is* its curse. I beg you,
turn away, and do not loose the evil
from its place of ambush.

Gawain:

The evil, ferryman?
Your speech grows still more puzzling. The maidens
look down on us, sad and mute, and I
somehow feel it is my own injury
that darkens their eyes. If I do not ask,
how can I hope to free my own affliction?

Ferryman:

O, there's no good counsel! I knew you'd wish
to try what none has e'er accomplished—
to free the maidens from their prison towers,
by confronting the foe no hero has e'er withstood,
no matter how strong his spear and sturdy shield.
For it is the art of Hell that blazes forth
in the castle; and if you approach, you will be
caught like a fly in the web of magic forces.
If you yourself do not know a higher magic,
the highest kind there is, you will fall
and sink in smoke and fire and sulphurous fumes,
and not a soul will know what happened at your end.

Gawain:

Hell is able to create such wondrous visions?

Ferryman:

It fashions it out of the maidens' pain, and dreams,
from the dim delusions of their innocence.
Take good measure, sir, of the danger!

Gawain:

Hell is mighty. I am no fool, I know
the strongest hearts may fall under its spell.
Still, are we not called by God to war against it?

Ferryman:

If the shield of your honor and your faith
is without fault, if your courage is the will
of heaven, if you know humility and, pure
in soul, never have abused the devotion
we owe to woman—then, noble Knight, then
there is hope; you may gain the victory.

Gawain:

God knows what I can do. I stand in answer
to the call of destiny. Therefore, tell me,
what is the castle called? And what mystery
does it conceal?

Ferryman:

Then know, noble sir,
the Castle of Marvels rises before your view,
the fort of evil, and the maidens whose dumb pictures
you have seen, live locked inside the towers'
golden cloisters, held by force of magic.
For this is the pain and shame and grievous harm
that humankind here suffers, that these pure,
innocent beings, whom the deadly light
of consciousness has not yet touched (for they dwell
still in dream) serve the sorcerer who, in cunning,
stole them. Thus he weaves his devilish tapestry
out of the mute threads of unlived lives,
twisting the enchanted yarns into the loveliest
of lies. Noble sir, do not believe the mirage
of beauty; the truth is spoken in the sorrow of their eyes.

Gawain:

Who is the blasphemer?

Ferryman:

The devilish sorcerer—Klingsohr.

Gawain:

So this is my enemy?

Ferryman:

Yes.

Gawain:

Very well, I will challenge him
with the sword of Heaven. Call the child,
so she can help me don my weapons.

Ferryman:

You'll venture battle with Hell's wizard?

Gawain:

I must.

Ferryman:

His weapons, child, his weapons!

Bene (*from without*):

I bring them.

Ferryman:

If you succeed in overcoming Klingsohr,
you'll not only become master of the castle,
but beauty then will form one league with truth,
and innocence be released from evil's thrall,
the forces of nature cleansed of all corruption,
and the anguish of illness offered healing.

Gawain:

So arm me, child! For the touch
of your hands will bless my sword and shield.

Bene:

Where are you going?

Gawain:

Where I must go: into
the Castle of Marvels.

Bene:

I will not part from you.

Gawain:

What do you mean, child?

Bene:

I will go with you.

Gawain:

Into the magic castle?

Bene:

Yes, sir, into every trial.

Ferryman:

Then I will myself not stay behind.

Gawain:

You too will come?
O you true, loving friends!

Ferryman:

You be true to us—true to the heavens
and to the world.

Gawain:

So come, let us venture it!

Scene 3 Castle of Marvels

A round chamber, crowned by a vaulted dome. In its middle, a snow-white, crystal-clear, round pillar rises up, its ribs running up to, and dividing the vaulted dome. The construction of the chamber represents the four elements. The blank floor, on which are inlaid plants, flowers, and animals, figures the Earth. Up to a certain height, the mosaic on the wall represents the watery realms with adventuresome fishes, undines, and sea-wonders; then, running in a ring around the room, another level represents the realm of air, with splendid, rare birds and flying creatures. The dome itself is the fire-realm.

In front of the pillar stands the mighty enchanted bed. It runs on crystal wheels and is decked with a green cover. Klingsohr is in front of the magic column and looks into it.

Klingsohr:

You, the greatest masterwork of my art
that makes the circumference of the world revolve
in marvelous dance around me, while images
fleeting as the breath of shadows wash
over your column's round transparency:
you, mirror of all that I am not,
you spying eye, you dragnet of my mind,
what do you show me in this early hour?
Ha, again comes a fool in arms, blinded
by the brilliant vision I myself created!
Do you crave to feel the force of my magic?
Hell itself has lent me its finest, most
murderous poison: veils, delicate as mist—
the maiden images have drawn you here,
for your fatuous heart thirsts after Love.

There, I'll catch you, for all love is death—
a wretched, agonizing end, mired
in desire, sunk in the pit of false pleasure.
What makes you stand so upright? You boast of virtue,
of manliness? Smote I not Amfortas
who seemed worthy to bear the weight of the Grail?
Did I not drive death's sting deep into his groin?
Does he not moan nights on end, screaming
for death? To die would be to live, but he
suffers living death, and this I prepare
for you, too, proud hero.

But what do I see? What company have you chosen?
The old Ferryman, whom I so hate, walks
by your side. My art can mock his wisdom,
but what goads and pricks me even more,
the child comes with him, the accursed one
who gapes with starry eyes about herself
and tears the veils of illusion with her smile.
Well, let them come. Who enters this hall
shall not leave before he triumphs— or falls.

You spirits, arm yourselves! Gather round!
(*The spirits form a circle around him.*)
Make thousandfold your weapons! Earth, Water,
Air, and Fire: prepare to display your power.
From your invisible battlements, pour ruin
and fell destruction down upon his head
like hail in storm; swell the dread nightmare
of his sense with a thousand fearsome dreams.

Spirits of Earth, yours be the solid space:
take hold the love-bed, hurl it around
and, thundering, shatter all his limbs.

Spirits of Air, from the canopy's high sweep
throw stones and spears and lightning down
so thick, that Death itself will take him.

You Water-Spirits, foam with wild desire;
swallow him in your raging tempest's waves.

You Fire-spirits, pour out fire and flame
and eat the breath from out his gaping mouth.

And if, after all this, he still resists
I myself will strike him down.

Veil yourselves! The horn calls us to the game!

He blows on his magic horn. The earth-spirits surround the magic bed, the water-spirits form a ring around the rim of the room, the air-spirits ascend to the balcony in the heights, the fire spirits appear in the dome. At the sound of the horn, the collected spirit-groups are hidden in mist and disappear. From the ground of the room, in the middle, a cloud of mist rises up and hides Klingsohr and the magic column. The chamber lies empty and still.

Gawain, the Ferryman, and Bene enter.

Gawain:

You call this, good friend, the Hall of Wonders?
It certainly appears wondrous in its splendor,
yet I cannot see anything evil in it.
The high chamber shimmers on every side
projecting restful pictures of the elements:
the earth's hard ground, the water's cool waves,
the airy realm, filled with wings of song
and the fire's noble, sun-like glow.

Ferryman:

Have care about you! It is the hall of death!
All that have tread this ground before
were lost, and carried out lifeless corpses.
For the elements appear before you here
spellbound, transfixed in dumb images.
But woe, if their nature be unchained
and their spirits rise up, thundering.

Gawain:

Man is the master of the elements
for he is chosen as their head, and heart.

Ferryman:

And yet to test if he is truly master,
they will unfold the wildest of their forces;
primeval chaos will suddenly re-appear
to try him to the limit of his strength.

Gawain:

A bed stands here, and beckons one to rest.
I will lie down upon it and wait
and see what more may happen here.

Ferryman:

Do it not, my lord, I warn you. This bed
that so peacefully invites your rest
brings you to ruin, if you light upon it.

Gawain:

To ruin? Shall I, who smote down heroes,
find myself in fear before a bed, good friend?

Ferryman (*to Bene*):

Child, dissuade him from it! You are silent?
Girl, have you entirely lost your tongue?

Gawain:

How can I triumph
if I dare nothing? Stand aside, friend.

Ferryman:

Only don't touch the bed!

Gawain:

Somehow, I must wake
the magic that lies sleeping here, must force
it out of hiding, so I can finally glimpse
its ghastly face.

Ferryman:

May the Lord our God then save you!
Come, dearest child! (*They move back and to the side.*)

Gawain:

Hide what you will; here
on your pillows, I will lie down.
(*The bed moves back away from him.*)
You shy
from the master that seeks you? Like a head-
strong horse, you try to dodge my will?
Run where you will, I'll catch you. For if
you evade my arms, you'll not escape—my Self.
(*Gawain springs onto the middle of the bed.*)

I have you!

Ferryman:

Pray, child; now all hell breaks loose!

(*A thunderclap. Fire and smoke stream from beneath the bed, which shudders. The scene darkens suddenly. Amidst the growing chaos, the bed rolls crazily, like a thing possessed.*)

Choir of the Spirits of Earth:

Break now the fetters,
the iron-clad bands
tear yourself, thundering,
from sleep's cold chain.
The wild awakening
of precarious power,
the roaring arousing
of giant desire—
Will rising heavenward
rearing and hurling
rock after rock
ruin upon ruin.
Fire in chasms,
fire in clefts
leaping like fountains
glowing in flame.
Deep in the abyss,
vaults of earth crumble,
sending rumbling thunder
through the shivering ground,

heralding Spirits of Earth's
unfathomed force.
For we desire
to become bodies,
and seek after your own
O Man!

(Many rolling thunderclaps. Thick smoke rises up; the hall itself shakes in apocalyptic uproar. After the climax, the uproar subsides. At last, weak murmur of thunder, and the smoke disappears; it becomes clear and light once more. Gawain, covered by his shield, his right arm holding his drawn sword, lies upon the bed.)

Bene (*softly, fearfully*):
Does he live?

Ferryman:
Quiet! Quiet!

Gawain:
Does the earth still stand?
The abyss yawned and the ravening flames
consumed the world. I dreamed the last days
of man dawned in dread apocalypse. Yet look:
the hall that sways before my dizzied sight
is all at peace. (*He sits up.*)

What sounds? A battle cry. Does the dance
begin only now?

(With the ongoing crescendo of the magic horn, there rises a blustering roaring that gradually intensifies to the howling of a hurricane. The bed-covers swirl up; all carpets, wall hangings, curtains, etc. are lifted by the wind; mist and clouds boil up on all sides and fill the chamber up to the balcony. In the rising of the fog, the whirling vortex of the element shows itself. Air spirits appear, shooting through the mists in demonic forms; they grab Gawain, lift him up and throw him back on the bed.)

Choir of the Spirits of the Air:

The soft air's
swerving singing,

the gentle roar's
growing swell
heralds the Spirit's
powerful coming,
heralds the host's
fast-stirring storm.
Here is no cover
over or under,
hither and thither
whips the whirl-wind.
Out of the void
powerfully springing,
out of the void
drawing ever more power.
Crowd of unfettered things,
crowd of hurrying wings,
unloosing everything—
ravening crowd!
Tearing through fastenings,
braces and bindings;
branches of law
breaking in two.

Lance and spear-flings,
arrows and slings,
hail and lightnings
rattle out loud!
Freedom in whirling,
riot and reveling,
making everything nothing,
desire wild and proud!

(*For a moment, the armed spirits appear along the parapets, and take aim at Gawain with their arrows. A thick hail of stones, then a stream of fiery shots rains down upon him. Gawain covers himself with his shield and remains lying motionless. The bed and his shield are peppered with arrows, which stick up like a forest of thorns. Gradually, the riot fades and quiets, and all is as it was at first. Gawain lies stretched out as if dead.*)

Bene (*as before*):
He stirs not.

Ferryman:

Be still, this was but
the second trial.

Gawain (*lifts his head*):

I am. The air-spirits
did not kill my own. They struck me
with sticks and stones, and sowed in my body
the hot seed of pain, and yet warm blood
still runs in my veins. And this briar-patch
in which I lie as if it were a bed,
I'll mow down with my unsheathed sword.

(*He does so.*)

I know now the earth, the air's course
as well. Will now the water reveal itself?

(*A giant fishman emerges with a trident. Klingsohr's horn sounds. The fishman knocks with his trident on the doors, and a flood flows out, filling the hall while the sound of crashing waves thunders forth. Many sea-monsters rush Gawain; soon, he's completely surrounded by them.*)

Choir of the Spirits of Water:

Roll around, roll around,
beat down with surges,
iron-cold urges,
everything down!

Roll around, roll around
swirl into whirl-
pools and pull
Everything down!

Roll around, roll around,
heavy with foaming,
roiling, seething,
pull everything down!

Now heap the waves up!
Our arms enclose all,
giving and yielding,

swelling and surging,
all the way round you,
as if they'd bound you;
you're but the toy of faceless force.

Dazzling and crashing,
spraying and splashing,
luring and stuttering,
lulling and laving,
foaming and muttering,
roaring and raving—
gurgling, growling,
glassily hollowing,
piling up, hovering,
quickly, you cov'ring—
suddenly circling,
with dizzying whirling,
fast in the funnel,
swallowing you up—
spitting you out—
throwing you through
the crystal spout—
'til wave upon wave,
rising in strife,
crashes and crushes
your trembling life.

(During the whirling dance of the water-spirits, Gawain remains motionless beneath his shield, knowing that the strength of the water element only increases when it is opposed by force. However, when the fishman then approaches him with his trident, Gawain rises.)

Gawain:

Is it thus? Come on!

Fishman:

Cursed fool! He does not know fear.
We can do no more. (*raising the trident*)
Back to the depths!

Gawain:

Water cannot drown courage. Yet listen,
the Horn! The fourth act begins.

(Klingsohr's horn sounds as before. The dome is filled with fiery flames that rain down upon Gawain on the bed. They cover the bed, the floor, climb the walls, build pillars of fire and hanging fabrics of flame in manifold shapes.)

Choir of the Spirits of Fire:

*Whirling tongues! Sing stronger, sing higher;
all's food for the ravening fire;
all is destruction and light.
Gather together, build up the choir!
Oceans of flame leap with desire;
beat against the hold of night.*

*Wings scorch and singe, arms fall back,
eyes extinguish, words sigh, and crack;
all that is husk will die; it cannot stay.
Never will you withstand the burning sear.
Are you but husk? You'll perish, and disappear—
husk's but ash, and ash will blow away.*

(*The rain of fire ends.*)

Gawain (*rising*):

The pure heart, like the salamander
is transfigured, not devoured, by glowing flames.
Is this now the end?

Ferryman:

Caution, great warrior!

Bene:

Caution!

(A long sustained threatening drumming swells through the room. In the middle of the room, a powerful cloud gathers that immediately begins to

glow from the inside out. As the cloud opens up, Klingsohr appears in the highest rage, magic staff in hand.)

Klingsohr:

Here I am, enemy. Disarm me
if you can. I cast a curse upon you,
the curse of the deepest, most hideous hell.
Here, this staff, with which I woke the spirits—
may it meet you, and deliver you to death.

(*He holds up the staff, and a lightning bolt streams out to strike Gawain's head; Gawain lies, shattered, on the ground.*)

(Bene throws herself forward, lifts Gawain's head, and whispers a word in his ear.)

Gawain *(with effort, snatches himself up, lifts both arms high, and calls loudly):*

Mary-Sophia, Diviner of Darkness!

(The floor opens up, a flame ascends, Klingsohr gives a loud cry, and sinks away. All signs of the battle vanish. Gawain lets his arms fall, reels, and collapses. Bene catches him; his head lies in her lap.)

Ferryman (*on his knees by the fallen Klingsohr*):

Thank God! Hell is conquered!
(*rising*)
Does he live?

Bene (*having taken off Gawain's helmet*):

He breathes, though he does not move. His face
is white as snow. Bring help, father!

Ferryman:

Your kerchief! (*Bene hands it to him; he hurries off.*)

Bene:

You lofty head now sunk in pale senselessness,
you noble brow, you lips like to petals
barely moved by breath's soft breeze,
O martyr of love, brave mimic of death,
you've founded woman's innocence anew,

closed the immemorial cleft of her heart
with the burning flow of your own wounds—
broken the old spell, and freed our blood
from the taint of ancient poison. Now you lie
snow-white upon my lap, soon to awaken,
the master of Hell's glittering marvels.
In the name of womankind, I thank you
with these tender, ne'er before touched lips.
(*kisses him*)

Ferryman (*returns with the cool, wet kerchief, and places it on Gawain's brow*):
Wake, hero, and open your eyes.

Gawain:
Where am I?

Ferryman:
In the place, where you have triumphed.

Gawain:
The enemy? Give me my sword. . .

Ferryman:
The fight is done.
Your head rests in Bene's lap.

Gawain:
You dear, true friends!
Help me to the bed; my limbs are weary.
(*They help him to the bed.*)
Klingsohr. . .

Ferryman:
...is fallen. The hell-spirits he commanded
followed him, shrieking, into the abyss.

Gawain:
The castle?

Ferryman:
Is wholly yours. You have redeemed it.

Gawain:

But the women?

Ferryman:

Even now, the queen and her retinue approach.

(Queen Arnive carries salve-oil in a gold vessel. Itonje follows her with a goblet; the other maidens follow. They form a circle around Gawain. Bene kneels at his head, the ferryman at his feet.)

Choir of Women:

Blessed be the man, the pure of heart,
strong in faith and in courage unbowed
who pledged his life to make us whole again,
redeeming us from grief, and grievous shame.
Pure is the earth, our feet now walk upon;
pure the water, that moistens and cools us;
pure, too, the air our lips drink in breath,
and pure the fire, that burns upon our hearth.
Whole is the body, whole the Life, and Soul,
whole the heart, long steeped in pain.
O new day— o hour of fresh joy,
o'er us the light of a new heaven breaks.

Arnive:

Still are you weak, you pinnacle of power;
still are you sick, you hearth of all health.
Raise your head, and take this healing draught
from us who greet you in love and gratitude.
(*She beckons to Itonje, who lifts the cup to Gawain's lips.*)

Gawain:

Thanks, noble queen. And you, fair cup-bearer.
And all of you maidens, greeting and thanks. . . .
(*Gawain falls into a deep healing slumber.*)

Arnive:

He's held in healing slumber. Soon he'll awake
with new strength. We'll go hence, and ready
the castle to receive him in fit form.

(*She leaves with the maidens; only Itonje remains behind, gazing at Gawain.*)

Itonje:

I cannot leave his side, for his fair features
touch me with a strange, familiar sweetness,
and remind me of a long-forgotten home.
I was stolen from my father's house
as a child; and every trace of memory
sunk as in the blackness of a well,
but now the distant images climb wonderfully
up the long dark shaft, barely veiled
in the mind's fine mist: my father's castle
and his face; and Gawain, my brother's, tender voice.
I scarcely saw him; before I was born, he served
King Arthur's court; once only, he came home,
lifted his little sister upon his arm,
gazed upon my face, kissed me, and said:
Itonje, little flower— alas, they signal,
I must go. Why did it happen thus to me?
Itonje, little flower—

(*She throws herself on her knees and kisses Gawain's hand, which is hanging down from the bed.*)

Yes, I am coming! (*hurries away*)

Gawain (*awakens*):

You, friends, watch over me? How well I feel!
My wounds and weariness—as if blown away.
(*rises*)

Bene, you called me to myself, when I
was already fallen. The maid accomplished,
what the man could not. My thanks, you treasure!
(*embraces her*)

And you, true friend, my guide and ferry
across the river of death's shadows: my thanks!

Ferryman:

Now I may say what I have long kept silent.
You are the only one who could have fulfilled
this task since the greater one rode silently past.

Gawain:

Say, which greater one?

Ferryman:

The one whom from land to land,
quick tongues call the red knight.

Gawain:

What, Parzival? He was at this place?

Ferryman:

The night before you, he slept in my house.

Gawain:

Alas, what strange design! To find you
I rode into this wilderness; restless friend,
will I never reach you? The enchanted castle,
did he not see it?

Ferryman:

His only question
was for the Holy Grail. Towards it was turned
his heart's whole longing.

Gawain:

O friend, O friend, the candelabra's torn
out of the hand of the cunning blasphemer.
Now bring the flame, that shall burn in it!

(*notices the magic column*)

What do I see here? What wonderful scenes—
a spectacle beyond compare! The world that lies
beyond these walls, imaged in the column.
Valleys, streams, and villages; the magnificent
rise of noble mountains; and there, along
an emerald river, a quiet and secluded grove
that in its solemn, yet fair and festive, dress
seems a place in Paradise, a very Eden.
And in the middle, shining, leaved with gold
a laurel tree with rounded crown, proud house
of the sun. Yet now, from out the shadows
of the wood, there ride a host of knights
and in their midst, a woman all made, it seems,

of brilliance. She turns, and shows her face...
it is she, the fairest! Orgeluse—
She lifts her arm; her red lips speak
some proud word; her brow sinks down;
the circle of knights around her rides away;
the fair one dismounts her palfrey, all alone.
She kneels on the ground, and hides her face
with both hands. Is she weeping? O Gawain,
how can you stand here like a child, charmed
by this fair picture-show, this light-play
mirroring truth? Have you had enough
of image? Will you lie still in dream
even as your awakened heart calls for action?
Into the saddle! Orgeluse calls and you must to her.

Ferryman:
I beg you, noble sir, rest
your limbs after your tremendous battle.

Gawain:
I, rest? Hand me my helmet, and my sword!

Ferryman:
You'll ride off?

Gawain:
Yes, and without delay—
yet will return, as master of the castle.

Ferryman:
I'll not hinder you. Yet there remains
one more act you must perform here.
Klingsohr laid so deep a spell upon this castle
that to enter into it is, indeed,
no hard task; and yet, once inside,
it holds you fast, and will not let you leave.

Gawain:
And is there is no way out of this mousetrap?

Ferryman (*points to a ring, secured by a chain to the magic column*):
Break the ring! Tear that chain!

Gawain (*lifting his sword*):
Thus, I'll break
the final spell. For a still greater work
awaits me. (*breaks the ring*)

ACT V Giromelans

Scene 1

A meadow by a river. On the far side, Giromelans' grove with the golden laurel tree. The river ford is to be imagined in the background, outside the scene.

Orgeluse: (*on her knees on the ground*)
Lischoys Gewelljus, the boldest of men
has fallen, and he, who cast him down, rode on
into the Castle of Marvels, the devilish death-trap
no man has e'er escaped—so he, too, is gone.
But what pains me yet more deeply, is:
there is one who desires nought of me,
who, denying my entreaties—not,
indeed, with coldness or with scorn, but drawn
as if in dream on towards the Grail—
leaves me in complete distress. Whom
can I now call upon to right my wronged
heart? Who will leap o'er the river to win
a sprig of laurel from the tree of my old foe?

Gawain:
Greetings, proud one! Since you flew from me,
my heart has sought you without rest.

Orgeluse:
Whence do you come?

Gawain:
From the Castle of Marvels,
where I have broken the ring of Klingsohr's power.

Orgeluse:
And he?

Gawain:
Is gone—his spirit driven to the depths.

Orgeluse:
    The magic bed?

Gawain:
    I tamed its restlessness.

Orgeluse:
    The tempest of elements?

Gawain:
    Silenced by me.

Orgeluse:
    Then are you master of the castle's wonders?

Gawain:
    The women there have welcomed me as such.

Orgeluse:
    So puff yourself up! Amidst the racket of spirits
    you've withstood the clever conjurer
    who fights with nought but things that seem, weapons
    of illusion, insubstantial and empty as air.
    You have conquered no-thing, you great some-thing!

Gawain:
    It was said, that no few had lost their lives
    in the castle. And so I ventured mine.
    Does this seem so unworthy to you, woman?

Orgeluse:
    As I told you, you should puff yourself up
    like the preening cock, who ruffles his feathers
    whilst casting sidelong glances here and there
    to see who's marveling at his unmatched prowess.
    What will you do now?

Gawain:
    I have hurried here,
    to serve you. The shame you foretold for me
    missed its mark; I have, meantimes, performed
    some work, and now ask what more may please you.

Orgeluse:

What more may please me? Never to see you more
would please me most, you cock-a-doodle-doo!
But as you show yourself so industrious,
do me yet one favor more, and leap
over the river on your horse, and from
the garden harbored there, on the far side,
bring back a branch from the laurel's golden crown.

Gawain:

You mean, that I should leap the river— there?
The water is uncommonly deep and wide.

Orgeluse:

So, the elect hero, the maiden-saver,
the smoke and mirrors master, finally shows
his true colors. Did you not pass the grand trial?
The river is water. Do you fear water, then?
The common opinion that, in it, one could drown?

Gawain:

I'll ride.

Orgeluse:

Good. But not here. Yonder, look,
there is a bank, steep, where the shores
press more close together, yet still leave room
for art, and whosoe'er misses his leap there
will be whirled down to watery depths.
There, leap o'er. I will await you.
And if you bring me the sprig I so desire,
I'll will give you a hair from out my horse's
piebald mane. Go, and do not delay!

(*Gawain rides toward the indicated spot.*)

He rides, and dares sheer madness, a deed that none
before have ventured. He'll fall and plunge
into the swirling waves, and all is lost.
O woe, that I must do, what I so hate,
sending all who woo me to ruinous death.
He's reached the place, takes a running start—
Ha! how horse and rider catapult themselves
from off the rocks! Too short! They hit the waves!

And sink! o God!

(*weeping and wringing her hands*)

His shining face, O his eyes,
quick messengers of the sun, so mild
and fair. Alas, all gone, all forever gone!

But look, he raises himself, wrestling, out of the waves
and catches hold of the bank on the far shore—
is it madness, or do I see man and horse
safely landed? Oh, my senses swirl
and dizzy, all I see—is reeling phantom...

(*She sinks unconscious to the ground.*)

(*Gawain, leading his horse behind him, appears in the garden on the far side of the river.*)

Gawain:

I sank, a dead weight, beneath the waves,
yet God's hand lifted me like a little child
from out a spluttering bath. (*kneels*)

We are nought; all work is yours, and if
I break a bough from off the golden laurel,
let it be, in your praise, and honor!

(*rises to break a branch from the laurel*)

(*Giromelans appears, unarmed, with a falcon on his fist. He is blond and shining, and his clothes carry emblems of the sun.*)

Giromelans:

Who dares to enter into this garden
the last refuge of holy paradise,
whose strict guard I myself am charged to keep?
Who broke a bough from off the Tree of Life,
which belongs to none but the great healer
through whom mankind's misery is ended?
Who are you, brazen warrior? What fierce madness
drove you on to such a wanton deed?
For the penalty you now must pay, is death.

Gawain:

If you would take my life, be forewarned:
my sword has subdued more than human power.

Giromelans:

What! How arrogant! Were I now in arms
I'd not hesitate to raise my sword and crush
your vain trespass. Yet it is not my wont
to go about the garden armed, for none has ever
dared to cross the rushing river until now.

Gawain:

Know me, then. As this sword conquered Klingsohr
it might parry your more human blows, as well.

Giromelans:

What, you o'ermastered Hell's spirits?
—are now called lord of the marvelous castle?

Gawain:

So it is.

Giromelans:

The women, your fair legion?

Gawain:

Yes.

Giromelans:

So tell me, proud warrior, your name.

Gawain:

I am Gawain.

Giromelans:

Gawain! The one whom
a dream once named my greatest enemy,
whose coming I have yearned for night and day
so we might resolve our still unsettled fates
by a fight unto the death. Welcome, hero!
Let it be, that one of us shall rise
even as the other falls. Let us pledge
to mortal battle.

Gawain:

If you so demand,
I'll not demur. Gawain's sword was never shy.

Giromelans:

Still, let's not hurry blindly to this work,
for such a contest should take place in view
of a host of worthy knight and ladies.
So let us, after a span of sixteen days,
meet again upon the field of Ioflanze,
whilst each invites the noblest and fairest of his land
as retinue, to witness the fight that shall decide
whether you, or I, are most fit to be
guardian of the Tree of Life for all future time.
But stay— there is one thing more I'd ask of you:
though you be my foe, still am I bound
to you by a bond of blood, most wonderful.
For she, for whom my heart yearns, and whose gain
is my highest wish, dwelt in Klingsohr's castle,
the dear, beloved Itonje, your fair sister.
Bring her this ring from my finger,
and give her greeting in the name of her hero.

Gawain:

I will do it. But tell me then, your name
so I may say from whom I bear the message.

Giromelans:

Giromelans.

Gawain:

Good. Live well.

Giromelans:

Will you go?

Gawain:

Yes.

Giromelans:

Which way, then?

Gawain:

The same, by which I came.

Giromelans:

Live well, Gawain; remember your word! (*exits*)

Gawain:

Itonje lives! Itonje at the castle!
O, of all wonders, the greatest, and most dear!
Yet, which of all the maidens may then have been
my sister? Like a crown of stars I saw them
circled round me— yet the fair cupbearer. . .
Itonje, dearest, O Itonje, mine. . . .
(*rides out, towards the other side of the river*)

Orgeluse (*rising out of unconsciousness*):

Ah—the green and festive fields so lately sunk
in oblivion spread before my wakened eyes
once more; the waters whose fierce force
flooded the portals of my mind, recede.
I journeyed far, fleeing through the dark chasm
towards a light that shone with ineffable clarity.
There, I sank in silence. Consumed in radiance,
all which had been mine, hate and love,
died there, and a boundless calm
washed over me, washed over the bottom
of my heart, which had been the abyss of heaven.
It was the place of the sun, and a hand
clasped a bough, bent it, and said: become!
And said: be! And said: yes, yes, yes; you are.
Where is Gawain?

Gawain: (*rides from behind slowly towards Orgeluse, branch in hand*)

Greetings, proud Orgeluse.

Orgeluse:

O, do not name me thus. I am not proud;
I am a woman who kneels upon the earth,
and prays.

Gawain:

What is it with you? The health of the sun
breathes within this golden laurel bough
which I broke for you. Receive it! Rise!
(*swings himself off his horse and approaches her*)

Orgeluse:

I'll not stand. Upon my knees, O sir,
I implore you—do not despise the maid
who so reviled you. For look, she—
I—have died, and now am born anew,
a child who longingly weeps for the arm
that will lift her. O Gawain, raise me!

Gawain (*raising her*):

Beloved! Take the branch of life, take it!
For it was plucked for no one, but yourself.
The one I love, shall never appear unworthy.
I knew you then, when you—O rose—still hid
yourself in thorns.

Orgeluse:

O you saw
into the depths of my soul, suffered the scorn
I poured unceasingly upon you, in silence.
I trembled— shook with fear— at every sentence
I pronounced, praying that you would not
turn your face from me in anger, and forever
banish me from the province of your heart.
O believe me, never did a woman suffer
as I suffered—for you, for the sacred dignity
of man, which seemed to me forever lost
since Giromelans killed Cidegast, my beloved
husband. O I had a tender heart, soft
as new-warm wax, but when the dearest of men
lay there—his hair, a bloody tangle, his cheek
caved in, his glassy eyes staring
with clouded gaze into awful emptiness
and no word of mine could ever call him back—
then my heart turned within my breast,
and Man and Murder seemed to me one
and the same. Then I swore never to rest
until I had found the man who was
no murderer, whom the strangling grip
of vengeance could not hold, and who—turning
death aside—would leap the flood to win
the sprig of laurel colored by the sun.
Each man who approached, I thus spurred on

to the test that would prove, or destroy him.
For weak is woman, when she loves what's weak,
dishonored, when devoted to what is miserable;
and to choose, what cannot pass through
the dark portal, is to invite death itself
into the bridal chamber of the heart.

Gawain:

Beloved!
But did not God salve your wounded heart?

Orgeluse:

I did not know him. And more,
is not redemption demanded of us, as well?
If God performed the act in human form
must then the *human being* not complete
the deed in guise of God? And is not the man
whose virtue serves, but does not succumb, to woman
not truly *human*? Do we not, at last, tempt men
so they will reveal who they really are?
For woman's love longs not only for the man,
but—far more—for the *human being*.

Gawain:

In human garment, God brought us healing.
We all strive, to find our divine raiment.
Yet there is one, whom the Grail has called. . .
but Hell is jealous of that man, and threatens
to devour him.

Orgeluse:

Who is it? Giromelans?

Gawain:

No, not he. He guards, what is past.
No future blooms within his garden; the Grail
will replace it in the middle of its realm.

Orgeluse:

Who then?

Gawain:

He has crossed your path.

Orgeluse:

The red knight!

Gawain:

Parzival.
Voices led him to Monsalvasch, the castle
of the Grail, that he might heal the wound
that tortures Amfortas, its long-suffering King.
Yet Parzival was silent when he should have spoken
and so was banished in disgrace. Lost
and yet still chosen, he now strays in darkness.

Orgeluse:

Woe! It was I that led Amfortas on to suffer
Klingsohr's thrust—the shaming spear that bit
into his groin. And that red knight, Gawain (for I
will tell you all), seemed to me so powerful,
I offered him my lands, I offered him
my love, if he would win the laurel wreath
from Giromelans' jealous hand. But he looked at me
with unseeing eyes, shook his head,
and rode on.

Gawain:

Your courting does you nought
but honor, for he is the greatest, and yet most
unhappy man, bearing in his outcast state,
the lot of us all. Let us clasp him to our hearts,
dear one, and the overwhelming weight that presses
upon his breast—let us bear it in ours as well
until the hand of heaven lift the burden
from us both.

Orgeluse:

So be it, dear one.

Gawain:

But we,
Orgeluse?

Orgeluse:

My name, my life, my being:
all these I give to you, my beloved Gawain. (*They embrace.*)

Scene 2 In the Castle of Marvels

Arnive:

Welcome, noble lord, and welcome, Lady.

Gawain:

The Duchess will make her home with us, Mistress!
Schloss Logrois, and the Castle of Marvels: these
two shall be as one, bound by ties of joy
just as these, our hands, shall soon be joined
forever.

Arnive:

Let me press you to my heart—
the beloved of our hero, you are loved here.

Orgeluse:

Given to him, I am yours, as well. *(They embrace.)*

Gawain:

Now be so kind, mistress, as to send
Itonje to me, the girl—unless I err—
who lifted the cup of healing to my lips.

Arnive:

Sir, I will bring her.

Gawain:

Good! Ask, too,
the ferryman, if he will follow after.

Arnive:

I shall.
And, if she so wishes, I'll now show
the Duchess the marvels of the castle.

(Arnive and Orgeluse exit; shortly, Itonje arrives.)

Itonje:

You called me, and I have come.

Gawain:

You are named—
Itonje? Who gave you this name, child?

Itonje:

My father, Lot.

Gawain:

I have heard well
of him—a noble man. Do you not have
a brother?

Itonje:

If he still lives, I have one, sir.

Gawain:

What is his name? But why do hot tears
start from your eyes? Have I wronged you
with my question?

Itonje:

Ah, no, pardon, it is
but longing. My brother's name—is Gawain.

Gawain:

And he is dear to you.

Itonje:

Yes, sir.

Gawain:

Is he,
perhaps, the dearest of all men known to you?
You are silent?

Itonje:

Sir, I cannot answer
that which you ask.

Gawain:

And yet you blush so deeply.
Child, believe me, I am a great riddle-master.

Itonje:

A riddle-master?

Gawain:

A word is imaged
in your eyes—and you cannot deny
its meaning.

Itonje:

I deny nothing.

Gawain:

Who sent you this ring?

Itonje:

Ring, sir?

Gawain:

Do you know the laurel-garden by the river?
Do you know the king, who there keeps watch?

Itonje:

Giromelans.

Gawain:

Only love speaks
so tenderly. Take this ring, and cherish it.
But that other, who—no less than he—
sent me to you, whose name I fear may be lost
amidst the quick fires of love—Gawain—

Itonje:

You know him?

Gawain:

Who asked me to discover
whether his sister's heart had not forgotten him—

Itonje:

O God, he lives! And you spoke to him?

Gawain: (*pulls her into his arms*)
Dearest,
in his name, I press you to my heart.

Itonje:
You are he! O brother! Brother! Brother!

Gawain:
For God's sake, dearest, do not die to me
again.

Itonje:
My heart bursts.

Gawain:
All the closer,
I press it to mine. Together, we'll bear
the excess of joy.

Itonje:
Let me go!
I can no more! (*She hurries out.*)

Gawain:
Itonje! O, my sister. (*The ferryman enters.*)

Ferryman:
Sir, I am here. What is it that you wish?

Gawain:
Good friend, I need your counsel.

Ferryman:
Ask, and I
will answer gladly, so far as I am able.

Gawain:
You warned me of a woman, who you said
wished me evil. I have decided to wed her.

Ferryman:
And I—what would you have from me?

Gawain:

To give me your opinion again, new-weighed.

Ferryman:

My opinion? Sir, that is not necessary.
The decision has been made.

Gawain:

For good, or ill?

Ferryman:

You ask me that? He who can transform
evil into good, truly, him I shall call master.

Gawain:

But how, my friend, can such a wonder happen?

Ferryman:

Who lowers mountains, who lifts the valleys,
so these and the highest peaks are one?
Who fills the night with shining and the day
with peace? Who robs the scorpion of its sting?

Gawain:

Love.

Ferryman:

Only love, and you may undertake
whate'er you will; it shall not fail.

Gawain:

Can the river's shores then be united?

Ferryman:

The bridge, that vaults them both, will do it.

Gawain:

The bridge, friend? So go, and build the bridge!

ACT VI Parzival

Scene 1

Early morning. In the background, the banks slope down to the river. From the river, thick mist arises, that alternatively veils and then reveals parts of the scene.

Gawain:

Now sport a while, brave steed, for today you'll fight
the great contest with me. The sun itself
is our prize, the garden filled with the blessings
of its radiance, the shine of past glory.
We'll strive to win the wreath of laurel, the sprig
of the Tree of Life, so Gawain may become
a new knight, one who heals, and does not kill.
But look how the fog rolls round us, rising
in ever thickening cloud from the river shore.
And what looms there, towering through the fog?
Woe, an angel!

Angel:

Gawain!

Gawain:

Who calls me?

Angel:

Climb from your horse!
It is fitting, that you fight on foot.

Gawain:

I obey.

Angel:

Gawain! Gawain!

Gawain:

What shall I—

Angel:
Bow to your destiny. (*vanishes*)

Gawain:
Bow? What oracle! Is my fall then fated?
(*The mist hides him.*)

Parzival:
There in the mist, I saw the watchman stand.
Now he's vanished. What shores do I tread?
Where does God's hand lead me?

Angel:
Halt, Parzival.

Parzival:
Who calls me?

Angel:
A fight awaits you.

Parzival:
I am ready. Command me, messenger!

Angel:
Dismount! It is fitting, that you fight
on foot!

Parzival:
I obey.

Angel:
Bow, bow to your destiny! (*vanishes*)

Parzival:
As God wills! (*The mist envelopes him.*)

Gawain (*stepping from the mist without his horse*):
I have glimpsed him. Like a phantom, he rose
from the river-bank, the shadow of the laurel
hovering o'er his helmet. I am not mistaken,
it is he, Giromelans! And if none of all

I invited here see us now, the destiny
that commands me, would have it thus. (*draws his sword*)

Parzival (*like Gawain, stepping from the mist*):
Whosoever you are, I am called to battle.
You draw your sword! So then, meet mine.

(They run with raised swords against each other and clash powerfully. The mist conceals them both. The noise of the battle recedes into the background. Iwanet feels his way through the mist in the foreground, comes to a standstill.)

Iwanet:
Where am I? From one mishap I stray
into another. All is lost—my horse
has fallen, and, for days, I have wandered
in this mist. But what sounds through the fog?
The din of weapons? O look, a shadow stumbles
out of the cloudy mist.

Gawain (*tumbling out of the mist*):
Woe to me!

Parzival (*following him*):
Meet the end, God has prepared for you.
(*With a sword blow, he strikes Gawain to the ground.*)

Iwanet (*crying out*):
Gawain! (*rushes to the side of the fallen Gawain*)

Parzival (*as if struck by lightning*):
Gawain? (*He throws his sword from him.*)
O the curse, that renews itself
whenever I lift my sword. Gawain! Gawain!
(*throws himself upon his knees and opens the visor of the unconscious Gawain*)

It is he. My brother. It is myself.
O God of Wrath, you have felled *me*.
Pale as death. His eyes vacant, and staring.

Beloved brother. Do not punish me! Wake up!
(tears his helmet from his head and gives it to Iwanet)
Quick, water!
(Iwanet runs to the river.)
To strike you, o precious head,
this is the most terrible blow that Heaven
has struck through me. For you were more than I.
As long as you lived, my breath would not fail,
though the curse of men lay stone-heavy
upon me. O, that I have done this!
Once more the abyss opens its grim jaws—

Iwanet:
Water! Water!

Parzival *(bathing Gawain's brow)*:
God breathes life into this element.
He pours life into your limbs. If you so will,
O Lord, awaken him!

Iwanet:
He lives. My lord Gawain! *(grasps his hand)*

Gawain:
What is . . .? I lie, vanquished. You, Parzival?
Giromelans—where is he?

Parzival:
Brother!

Gawain:
Is he no longer here?

Parzival:
What, brother?

Gawain:
He who struck me down, Giromelans,
Lord of the laurel garden.

Parzival:
He was not here.

Gawain:

Not here?

Parzival:

He who met you here
was I.

Gawain:

You?

Parzival (*embraces him*):

Brother, dear, true brother!

Gawain:

You felled me? Ah, so the blow will do me good—
was a love-tap. To be defeated by you
is good. Take my renown, O great one,
and place it in the crown around your head.

Parzival:

How fare you?

Gawain:

Well. High-spirited as after death.
I gave you what I have; we are one.

Parzival:

You will recover.

Gawain:

Friend, I am well.
Let me stand up. Ah, I'm dizzy yet.
Yet you are mine. I sought you full of longing.
Now you've given me the blow that makes us brothers.

Parzival:

You are not angry?

Gawain:

With him whom I love?

Parzival:

O, you are too good!

Gawain:

Only God is good.
Do you seek the Grail?

Parzival:

I am patient.
What God gives me, I accept in silence.

Gawain:

He gave you, me. Take it. The enchanted castle
is now mine. Innocence, redeemed.

Parzival:

You have won the Castle of Marvels, brother?

Gawain:

Klingsohr's driven hence, the women, freed.
And Orgeluse, whom Amfortas, against the will
of the Grail, sought to serve, will be my wife.

Parzival:

She, too, you have transformed?
O you have done much!

Gawain:

Take it, it is yours!

Parzival:

Mine?

Gawain:

As am I, myself.

Parzival:

And for this,
I had to strike my noble brother's head?

Gawain:

Speak no more of it. My strength increases
with every glance you give me. And look,
the faithful Iwanet, too, is returned to us.
Bring me my horse. Help me into the saddle.

Mount your steed as well, and let us ride.
For Giromelans has challenged me to battle
and it was he I thought to fight here by the river.
(*The mist abates more and more.*)

Parzival:
The battle's mine. I'll fight in your place.

Gawain:
That cannot be; to strive to win this prize
suits me alone.

Parzival:
Still, I'll not consent
that you stand against him thus, when you
have scarce regained the strength to stand and walk.
The battle shall be put off for one day.

Gawain:
To that, I can agree.

Parzival:
What glimmers there, along the forest edge?—
bright as flowers appearing through the mist.

Gawain:
King Arthur's camp. Him, and his host
I've invited as witnesses to the great contest.
We've already joyed much in our reunion.
Let's to him.

Iwanet:
O sir!

Gawain:
What is it, my child?

Iwanet:
Will you forgive me? I left you, for I thought
only thus would I be true. And yet
how wrong I was, I soon learned. I lost
my way, my horse—but God did not leave me.
For now, I've found you both.

Parzival:

You tore away
the veil, so I might see, whom I struck.
Your cry saved us.

Gawain:

Give me your hand, boy!
Here are both, to whom you've been loyal.
Whom, now, will you serve in the future?

Iwanet:

Sir Parzival needs no page. Will you
take me back?

Gawain:

Come with me!

Iwanet:

And, sir—a horse—

Gawain:

Will I give to you. Come, to the tents!

Scene 2 In Gawain's tent

Orgeluse helps Gawain put on his arms.

Orgeluse:

For my sake, you ride into battle, and so
with these weapons, I offer you—myself.
For when a woman gives a man his armor,
all that she possesses turns to his defense.
Fear then becomes courage; love, the glowing
ardor of the heart; humility, strength
and power. You fight for light, and for healing.
Let light and life shine in and through you, Gawain!

Gawain:

Beloved, a wonder is revealed to me.
I am man on the outside only, whilst within

in the center of my self, there kneels a woman,
clothed in purest white, bearing in her hands
the image of God. For woman is a prayer,
that hovers between the poles of our being—
near to Earth, and yet too, the familiar of Heaven.

Orgeluse:

And yet, we are whole only within man
whose deep power leads us down to Earth.

Gawain:

And yet, we are whole only within woman
who lifts us lovingly up towards Heaven.

Orgeluse:

To battle then, and triumph for us all.

Gawain:

In the will of God, and your deep trust.

(*Arthur and followers enter.*)

Arthur:

Gawain!

Gawain:

My King?

Arthur:

Loose the girdle of your sword,
Put off your weapons! Do not go to battle!

Gawain:

How so, my uncle?

Arthur:

All your friends,
speak with one voice, and say it shall be thus.

Gawain:

I shall not fight?

Arthur:

Yesterday, the mighty Parzival
cast you down. Your strength is not yet whole.

Gawain:

A night of sleep heals all.

Arthur:

Gawain, the blow
you took upon your breast, cannot be
so quickly overcome.

Gawain:

If Parzival
conquers me, my strength and honor's not at risk.

Arthur:

Defeat is defeat. The heart's an enigmatic master.
One's courage is shaken, even if you will not
confess it; a breach opened in the wall
of faith that encircles and guards the heart.

Gawain:

There is no breach.

Arthur:

Nephew—be warned.

Gawain:

You'll not dissuade me, uncle; the effort's in vain.

Arthur:

If the King's words weigh so little, then think
of the afflicton that torments your sister's heart.

Gawain:

Itonje?

Arthur:

Since she has discovered whom you would fight,
she cries unceasingly, weeps, and tears
her hair; her lament echoed all through the night.
Her poor heart—should it then lose her brother,
or should it lose her beloved, by the sword?

Gawain:

I cannot be cowardly.

Arthur:

You'd rather shatter
your sister's life.

Gawain:

Do not press me!
Doubt is my only enemy.

Arthur:

Go to Itonje; look at her, and see. . .
but what noise! There she is, herself.
(*Itonje enters, her hair loose.*)

Itonje:

Is Gawain here? O brother, brother, brother!
It cannot be. I will not suffer it; first
you'll have to run me through. For I will stand
upon the lists, and will not clear the way
"til both your lances pierce the heart already
cleft in twain.

Gawain:

Itonje!

Itonje:

You'll kill him I love,
and be his murderer, or he will kill
my brother, and come to me, a murderer,
to offer his strange, bloody hand? And forever
there hovers between us the threatening spirit
of my fallen brother? No, it cannot be.

Gawain:

Calm yourself, sister.

Itonje:

You gave me his ring,
you made yourself the messenger of our love.
Why did you not fling away the tainted token?
Why not shove me, rudely, from your arms?
Who offers the falcon and, as well, the knife
that pierces its breast? O awful, vain, love!

Gawain:

What's to be done?

Itonje (*clasping his knees*):

Do not fight, Gawain! Lay
your weapons down. Must you give the sword
the last word? Are there no other voices?

Knights (*from outside*):

Make way! Make way!

(*Giromelans is led in, tottering, with hacked helmet.*)

Itonje (*crying out*):

Giromelans!

Gawain:

Giromelans!

Arthur:

What's happened, King?

Giromelans:

A place to sit! I reel.

Itonje:

Dearest. . .

Giromelans:

Itonje! You are joy
and pain at once.

Itonje:

What has happened to you?

Giromelans:

I am defeated. Gawain—

Itonje:

What did Gawain—?

Giromelans:

—took my renown.

All:

Gawain?

Giromelans:

In the grey of morning,
as I practiced by the field of battle,
I met him—

Itonje:

Who?

Giromelans:

Your brother.
We charged each other, clashed in battle;
he threw me to the ground; all then came
to an end—

Gawain:

King, look up! The armor
of the hero, whom you fought, was thus?

Giromelans:

No. His armor was red.

Gawain:

Indeed. The one
who struck you down, is he, who vanquishes all,
before whose sword I myself have fallen:
Parzival.

Giromelans:

Ah—! So our time
is yet to come.

Gawain:

Yesterday, you put off
our battle for one day. Take a like
respite from me!

Itonje (*steps between them both*) :

No, heroes, no.
When the right hand shows itself thus hostile

to the left, when the swords held in both
cross murderously, then, in the brief rest
before the silver lightning strikes, the heart
steps in to guard the tender center. Then
every blow, from the left, from the right
meets its nakedness.

(*to Gawain*)

Beloved brother,
I'll not let you; your enemy, I will make
into your friend, as the flame will turn
coal into fire. For you do not love me
if you'll not offer your hand to him in peace.

(*to Giromelans*)

You, my beloved and my brother, I can allow
no more than I can that one there. Him
I'll make your friend, as the flame will turn
dark coal into fire. You do not love me
if you'll not offer your hand to make peace
between us all. For when two find themselves
within a third, they are made one. And so,
offer your hands and bury the enmity
that riddles all our hearts.

Gawain (*offering his hand*):
It shall be so.

Giromelans:
It shall be so.

Itonje:
I bind
your hands with the same golden band
and hold and protect all in my heart.

Giromelans:
Let the battle prize fall equally to us both:
the garden and the laurel be—Itonje's.

Gawain:
Yet two more hands will I unite here.
Forgive, and begin to honor one another.

(*He leads Orgeluse to Giromelans, and lays their hands together.*)

Giromelans:

I loved whom I struck down.

Orgeluse:

In my hate,
was love, as well.

Arthur:

So is illusion purged
from our hearts, and the clear sun, like
the light of truth, illumines all these deeds.

Giromelans:

Friends, today grace has returned to us all.
So let us celebrate a day of joy.
Defeated by the sword, we are yet victors.
Come with me; do me this honor, and fill
the table set before my tent, prepared
already, to host this day of triumph.
You, Arthur, and all your people, I invite;
you, too, Gawain, the hero who overcame
the black magician; and you, Orgeluse
who, transformed, stands before us shining
with such inner beauty that we all bask
in its radiance All ladies, all knights, come!
(*to Itonje*)
In your loosed hair, beloved, undone
in your distress, you look most like a bride
and will, as bride, walk by me, even
as Gawain and Orgeluse may now choose
so to crown their love. But the tears,
beloved, the tears you have wept, I will
with pearls and shining jewels far outweigh,
weaving a wreath of purest light round your head,
so you will sparkle like a thousand suns.
Unroll the banners of joy! Friends, come!

Gawain:

Go, loved ones, go. I will follow after
when I have changed this iron for fitter stuff.
Uncle, I give you Orgeluse.

(*Giromelans leads Itonje; Arthur takes Orgeluse's hand; all depart happily.*)

Gawain:

Strife is not the end; the end is silence,
surrender, and—peace.

(*Parzival enters in full armor.*)

Parzival:

Gawain!

Gawain:

Brother!

Parzival:

If I felled you yesterday, then today
I struck down your foe. Now it is clear to me
that I was led here, to perform these deeds.
Now all is done, I shall quit Ioflanze.

Gawain:

You'll go?

Parzival:

Yes.

Gawain:

You cannot linger here with us?

Parzival:

No.

Gawain:

Not share the joy, that shines upon us?

Parzival:

Joy shines not on me. I have no place
since my errant heart shut me out
of my true home.

Gawain:

You dwell in our hearts.
Do you not know that?

Parzival:

Good friend, cherish me still
within your bosom! Yet do not require
that I remain here. Live well!

Gawain:

You'll leave us?

Parzival:

To find you.

Gawain:

Your steps lead far
into the dark.

Parzival:

Into the dark light.
God speaks Yes and No. And I will listen.

Gawain:

Will you come back to us?

Parzival:

Do I know?

Gawain:

Without you, our building lacks the sacred dome.

Parzival:

God is the dome.

Gawain:

Yet the human being, too, curves this round.

Parzival:

The human being! Then let there be
the human being!

Gawain:

Live well! My heart is yours.

Parzival:

Live well! May you be blessed by the Holy Grail!

(Parzival exits. Iwanet enters and helps Gawain change his garments even as the final processional begins, as couples begin entering from the wings. Finally, Giromelans and Itonje emerge; lastly, Orgeluse joins Gawain; these two couples stand in the center, ringed by the gathered company. A Priest or Priestess speaks these words over them.)

Priest(ess):

And so be circled by the eternal ring.
For neither man nor woman is alone eternal;
this word belongs to the human being
and only the human being. Know, then,
this truth: He and She are no single thing,
but an All, embracing everything: the home-
coming of the soul's wide scatterings, the house
of joy. Let it be fulfilled!

(Giromelans and Itonje, and Gawain and Orgeluse, exchange rings and are wed.)

finis

PARZIVAL

Dramatis Personae

Parzival	Seeker of the Grail
Herzeleide	Parzival's mother
Ornite	Herzeleide's lady-in-waiting
Knights	Knights of the forest
Sigune	Parzival's cousin
Gurnemanz	Elder knight, Parzival's counselor
Liase	Gurnemanz' daughter
Castellan	
Conduiramur	Queen of Pelrapeire, Parzival's wife
Einhard	Conduiramur's steward
Manfiliot	Hermit, Conduiramur's uncle
Watchman	
King Clamide	
Amfortas	Grail King, Parzival's uncle
Fisherman	
Chamberlain	
Lance-bearer	Servants of the Grail
Black-clothed knight	
Grail knights, ladies, maidens	
Repanse de Schoie	Grail Queen, Parzival's aunt
Titurel	Great-grandfather of Amfortas
Kundry	Grail messenger
King Arthur	
Gawain	Knight of the Round Table, Arthur's nephew
Lady	
Knight	
Trevrizent	Hermit, Parzival's uncle
Feirifis	Parzival's half-brother
Trebuchet	Grail blacksmith
Angel Choir	The Nine-fold Spirit of the Divine

ACT I

ACT II

ACT III

ACT I

Scene 1 Herzeleide's Sorrow

In the Forest of Soltane, Herzeleide's Court

Chamber of the Queen. Night. Herzeleide before a chest. Ornite brings a light.

Herzeleide:

Bring the light here, Ornite. Hear—the wind!
Does Parzival sleep?

Ornite:

I was at his threshold.
It seemed that he was breathing deeply.

Herzeleide (*beckoning*):

So close the door!

Ornite (*closes*):

What do you wish, Herzeleide?

Herzeleide:

Know you not—
O know you not, what this night signifies?

Ornite (*falls at Herzeleide's feet*):

Ah, Lady!

Herzeleide:

Fourteen years ago; the candles
burned so still in the room as today,
the moonlight hung in shimm'ring veil.
O Konvoleis, you castle of death's pains!
They brought to me the torn and bloody shirt,
They brought to me the purple-reddish lance-point
that had fatally bored into his heart—
Do you still remember?

Ornite:

How shall I e'er forget it!

Herzeleide:

It is once more my lord's memorial day:
though not his death day—it is my own.

Ornite:

O wretched hour—do not speak of it!

Herzeleide:

For fourteen long years, no word of Gahmuret
has moved my mouth, and nameless was
my ev'ry sigh. Open up the chest.

Ornite:

God, you will not—

Herzeleide:

Open! I will dip my lips into his blood.

Ornite:

But Parzival—

Herzeleide:

He sleeps. The sleep of childhood
is deep, and angels stand around his soul.

Ornite:

But what if he awakens? Or what if a dream
reveals to him the ghostly spectre of this night?
Let the chest rest, the coffin remain closed.
You yourself have said: he may not see
the least sign of knighthood— no hint, no clue
should ruin the innocence of his eyes.

Herzeleide:

The sword is death: never shall he know
the sword. But I am entangled in this death;
you cannot deflect its sacred poison from *this* breast.
Open!

Bring forth the royal ornaments
with which I covered the holy sacrifice.
Give here the cloak, the crown. Lady Queen
of Sorrow let me be.

(She adorns herself with a queenly mantle and crown.)

Gahmuret, see your wife! My being has lived
in Parzival, our child; for to me, he became you
and every smile upon his lips— was you,
and every glance from his wild, self-willed eyes.
With this yearning that spans—shivering—every abyss,
I embrace you....

(*She kneels down before the chest and bows low, hiding her face in her hands. A loud knock at the door.*)

Ornite:

A knock! O heavens! heavens!

Herzeleide:

What is it?—Parzival!

Parzival's voice (*from outside*):

Quick mother, quick!
Open the door! Quick, I cannot wait!

Herzeleide:

The shirt! The lance! Hide them!
(*hides them in the trunk; hurries to the door and opens it*)

For God's sake, child, what is it?

Parzival:

The spear, Mother!
Give me quick the spear!
The bear is there again.

Herzeleide:

The bear?

Parzival:

That stole the honey just yesterday
from the little bee-house. (*presses into the room*)

Herzeleide (*deflecting him*):
Stop, child.

Parzival (*noticing her adornments*):
Mother, what is it then? What are these clothes?
I never saw you wear this cloak before.
And the bright band you're carrying in your hair.

Herzeleide:
The cloak and band are from an earlier time.
I'll take them off, and then be yours again.
Ornite, take them.
(*hands both to Ornite, who lays them in the chest*)

Parzival:
Mother, they look so well on you, and yet
you look so strangely. Why are you still
awake? Did the bear frighten you?

Herzeleide:
A bear, my boy,
does not scare your mother. Should he rob
the honey that he so likes out of the baskets
there's a still greater sorrow.
Ornite may now leave us; for today
her work is done. Child, stay here with me.

Ornite:
Sleep well, my mistress. (*departs*)

Parzival:
You look so strangely, mother....

Herzeleide:
Still so strange? O my child, the night
is different from the day, though in your youth
you cannot know this. Festively dressed
in the jewelry of stars, its sublime beauty
sinks into our hearts.

Parzival:
But if the honey's stolen from the hive—!

Herzeleide:

Then let it be. Come now, sit by me.

Parzival:

May I lie down upon your heart
as oft before? It has been so long.

Herzeleide:

The time is long past, when you, a child
loved to fall asleep upon my bosom.
You are almost a young man.

Parzival:

Still, I never slept so sweetly, mother.

Herzeleide:

Come, then, come to me.

Parzival (*on his mother's lap*):

Will it be so, forever?

Herzeleide:

Ah, be still, child!
Happiness flees more swiftly than a smile; softly
does God remove the veil from its splendor
and hides it once more quick and deep from sight.

Parzival:

Mother, who is God?

Herzeleide:

Do you not know him?

Parzival:

You never said a word of him. I know not
of whom you speak.

Herzeleide:

Ah, he is in you.
You know him well.

Parzival:

You speak so darkly.
You are in me. Is that then God?

Herzeleide:

Ah, no. God is radiant light.

Parzival:

A light?

Herzeleide:

A holy father.

Parzival:

A father—what is that?

Herzeleide:

O ask not, child,
for every word does wound my soul.

Parzival:

O woe, that this is so! Yet I must know
who God is.

Herzeleide:

Ah, how can I answer you?
He is more beautiful than any earthly being,
and great and almighty as the fire.

Parzival:

But how, mother, should I speak to him?

Herzeleide:

You holy angels, save me now from death.

Parzival:

That will I do.

Herzeleide:

But now let us rest.
The night is passing. I will take you to bed.

Parzival:

O let me stay here! Once more, sweet mother.

Herzeleide:

This one time, my child.

Parzival *(lying on her lap)*:

Sing me the lullaby—
the old one, that sounds so like a dream. I have
not heard it for so long.

Herzeleide:

O, child, do you wish to be mine as before—
O, how bittersweet! *(Tears well in Herzeleide's eyes.)*

Parzival:

Mother, sing to me.

Herzeleide (*pulling herself together*):

SONG Moon over Konvoleis

Moon, moon over Konvoleis, you silver sphere
From blue vaults you come gliding here.
The nurses are dreaming, the mothers are tending,
Wide, wide, the sea is unending.
Silver sea, silver deep,
Sleep, my little child, sleep.

Moon, moon over Konvoleis, you silver grail
what are you hiding there within?

The fog stirs in the vale;
I kiss my child's lamb-soft skin.
Silver sea, silver deep,
Sleep, my little child, sleep.

(Lights dim, Parzival asleep. As if in dream, two knights appear. The dream Parzival emerges from the darkness—young Parzival is still sleeping—and sees the knights.)

Dream Parzival (*sinking to his knees before the knights*):
Be greeted, shining God!
Be greeted, you angels on fair steeds!

Knight:
Boy, what are you saying? I am
not God. Nor are we angels.

Parzival:
What are you then?

Knight:
Servants of God. We are called knights.

Parzival:
Knights? Are you thus by your own power?
Have you made your own selves knights?

Knight:
No, child, a knight is not thus made.

Parzival:
Did God do so, then?

Knight:
Not God, either, child.

Parzival:
Who then?

Knight:
There is a king that is the model
and glory of all knighthood. His name
is Arthur.

Parzival:
He made you knights?

Knight:
Yes, child. Why do you ask?
Do you wish to become a knight?

Parzival (*repeats to himself*):
Arthur.....
How can I find him?

Knight:
Ride out of the forest
towards the sunset and ask in every place:
all will gladly tell the way.
(*dream fades: dream-Parzival, knights disappear*)

Parzival (*awakening*):
Mother, mother!

Herzeleide:
Don't be afraid.
What is it child? What have you seen?

Parzival:
I dreamt the most splendid thing my eyes
have ever seen. Men all made of light,
more beautiful than angels, riding through the forest.
The most beautiful, their leader, spoke to me
in a friendly voice, showing me the path
I might take to become splendid and light as they.
I'll take this path, I'll set out, tomorrow!

Herzeleide:
Child, tell me quickly,
these men you have seen, what were they called?

Parzival:
Knights!

Herzeleide:
Oh, this is the spear-blow reserved for me!
Now it is thrust home!

Scene 2 In Fool's Clothing

Herzeleide at a table. In front of her, the chest with scissors and sewing gear. Coarse sackcloth on her lap, that falls stiffly to the ground. She is working on an outfit for Parzival. Ornite enters, with rough calfskin, scissors for cutting leather, an awl, and laces.

Ornite:

Here's what you requested. Where's Parzival?

Herzeleide:

There he runs—madly—after his horse.
To him it is more than heaven, earth, and stars,
more than the heart that so pines for him.
He will not stay.

Ornite:

Gahmuret's seed—
could one expect anything else from him?
As soon as his clothes are ready, he will leave.

Herzeleide:

He does not hear me. He calls out Arthur's name
a hundred times a day. Like a magnet
this hero draws him.

Ornite:

You must let him go.

Herzeleide:

I'll let him go, if he will not stay.
Still, there may be one last means of turning
him back to us. Look!

Ornite:

That coarse cloth—
it's used only for sacks! But what
are you sewing out of it?

Herzeleide:

Clothes for Parzival,
a peasant-shirt, a fool's outfit—look there!

Ornite:

A true oaf-coat, as fat as it is foolish.
Like *that* you'll send Parzival out of his house?
With sheep-bells dangling from his tasseled cap?
So do clowns go wandering through the world.

Herzeleide:

And with that, a horse, as sorry as can be—
a clumper that would shame the poorest carter.

Ornite:

But why do this? Will not everybody
laugh at him? Pelt him with stones?

Herzeleide:

Thus—so alone, perhaps he will turn back.

Ornite:

In vain, Herzeleide. What he must be
he will become, clothed even as a fool.

Herzeleide (*rising*):

The shirt is done. The shoes are almost ready;
will you lace them?

Ornite:

There he comes, with his horse. (*Parzival enters.*)

Herzeleide:

Here are your clothes, rider! Try them on.

Parzival:

How strong and good! And for the rain, too,
the fine cap! With bells, even, you have nicely
adorned the top, the roof upon my head.
How can I thank you?

Herzeleide:

In that you think of me.
Now go inside and dress for the journey.

Parzival:

Such fine clothes! I am sure no knight
in all the land has such a suit as this!
(*goes inside with his clothes*)

Herzeleide:

O innocence, sweet innocence, how
the cold, graceless world will disdain you!
(*to Ornite, who is working on the shoes*)

Ornite:

Hardly pretty, and yet, it is a shoe. There—
it is ready.

Parzival: (*who has come back in dressed in his fool's outfit*)

And so is the rider. I'm ready to go!

Herzeleide:

Already?

Parzival:

Why should I delay?
King Arthur surely will be most glad to greet
a new knight at his castle! Why should I
keep him waiting any longer?

Herzeleide:

My only, my last....
wait a little, stay this last, poor hour.
It is your mother, who bore you, that asks you this.
I can't let you go 'til I have counseled you.

Parzival:

If you must,
then do it now. Look, the sun is rising;
it is time for me to go.

Herzeleide:

Sit on this stool. (*kissing his feet*)
Let me kiss these feet, then let these shoes
wrap and hide them, let me tie the laces
for the last time with the knotted bow
that you—alas, so soon—will undo
thus loosing the memory of your mother.
Be covered, you defenseless soles.
It is the earth, my child, that you tread.
'Til today, I carried you, but now
bless these soles that carry you further on your way.

Now, listen—it is a moment
that never will return, and my voice
you hear now for the last time.

Parzival:

Please, mother, do not speak like that;
I'll grow sad, and just now everything
is so happily ready for my journey.

Herzeleide:

Hear me, my son. If you cannot hear me
with your heart, listen with your ears,
and take with you the empty echo of these words.
The hour will come when their hollow ring
will fill with life, and meaning.
Perhaps you'll not come back, perhaps you will
as your father before you, become a knight.
Half of that which makes a knight, O
beloved child, a man can fitly teach you;
the other half, a woman only can reveal
for deeper still than Man is Woman, for she
is purity, and purity carries within itself
the image of God. Therefore, my dear child,
greet, as women do, all others kindly
and meet them with the shining light of love
so that they, like wanderers in the darkest night
that see above them the radiance of stars
will be reminded of the eternal world.
Do not ride through dark fords, where oft
depths are concealed by shadowing branches;

where clarity is, there cross over the stream
and so come safely to the other side.
To venerable elders, lend a willing ear
and be not angry if you earn a stern rebuke
from a greying head; for wisdom rests concealed
in the white snow of age. Think of the lovely
morning star; he who has glimpsed his radiance
cannot practice evil, nor be defeated
by the wants and confusions of his heart.
Choose this star, the pure one, for your guide!
Then God will give you the destiny that is yours.

And now, my child, if it must be, then go!
Take this kiss, the last, and think upon
these words I have spoken to you. (*She kisses him.*)

Parzival:
Live well, O mother!
Ornite, live well. (*Parzival goes out, departs.*)

Herzeleide (*goes after him to the end of the room, and stands there, motionless*):
God, great God, I give him
into Your arms, your eternal embrace,
hold him close to your heart.... (*She sinks down; dies.*)

Ornite (*crying out*):
Herzeleide!

Scene 3 Sigune: "Midmost Through"

A desolate spot, hemmed by somber woods, over whose old, withered crowns clouds pass. In the middle, a bare rock surrounded by thorns. Before it kneels Sigune with the corpse of Shionatulander on her lap. Her hair is in disarray, and she looks in wild despair down on him.

The entire scene is rather dark, only the rock and human figures are in dim light.

Sigune (*sings*):

Done, all is done. Since you,
my lord, my life, my beloved one,
before me murdered lie,
became all day a night; the green of earth,
the color grey of death, and everything flowing, ice.
Done, all is done.

(*speaks*) Over my soul fell the black veil
of death. My eyes are changed into a grave,
O beloved, you lie there dead;
your cheeks, your mouth, pale as flower petals
touched by frost's murdering hands.
Do you not hear me?
Will you not open your eyes,
so that I might feel the warmth of your gaze?
Will you speak no word of love,
as I have heard you speak so oft before?

(*crying out*)

Dead! Dead! Forever stiff and dead.
But still I live, and cannot die.
(*She covers the dead one; Parzival appears and approaches her.*)

Parzival:

Why weep you, woman? Who lies upon your lap?

Sigune:

The dearest and most brave of men.
There, behold him!

(*raises the cloth off the corpse*)

Parzival:

O woe, this knight
lies there, as once my mother lay,
devoid of sense and dumb.
Will he not soon awake?

Sigune:

Noble boy,
he wakes no more. See it, he is dead.

Parzival:

Dead? Can a knight be dead? I saw birds
die from my arrows, deer as well
and bear, as I felled them.
But people—woe! This I had never seen!

Sigune:

You child, you naive child! Has no one ever
told you of death, that everyone will die?

Parzival:

Ah, everyone? Say, have I heard aright?
Do you mean every person?

Sigune:

Yes, everyone

Parzival:

O woe! My mother too, and friends, and—you?

Sigune:

All these, as well as you, yourself.

Parzival:

O no, I will not die.

Sigune:

Child, foolish child,
what nonsense do you speak?
Do you not know the world is nothing more than death?
Who let you ride forth in idiot's clothes?
How are you called?

Parzival:

I have no name as other people do:
Darling, dear son, my child, sweet boy—
all these my mother and our servants called me.

Sigune:

Ah! Ah!

Parzival:

What is it?

Sigune:

Cherished child,
You are the dearest, most naive of children.
You, Herzeleide's son.

Parzival:

What, do you know my mother?

Sigune:

How should I not know the one who raised me once
in Konvoleis, she, the sister of
my own dear mother, too early passed away.
Child, we are cousins.

Parzival:

What is your name?

Sigune:

Sigune am I, this dead one's bride.

Parzival:

It cut my heart to the quick
when I saw you.

Sigune:

And did you ride away
from your mother's court, and did she
herself give you these clothes?

Parzival:

She has made them for me.

Sigune:

Ah, in her need! She wanted to protect you,
that you should not become a knight like Gahmuret,
your kingly father, and not like this one here
lying in the dust with bloody countenance.

Parzival:

Does she, as well, believe that I could die?

Sigune:

Silly boy,
she does not believe, she knows.

Parzival:

Still, I ride without pause,
that I may be a knight; I must become one.

Sigune:

Alas, there speaks your father
through your mouth. Your mother's heart broke
when he died, as my own did break
when my beloved fell. Deeply did the thrust meet her,
midmost through. Turn about, child!

Parzival:

No, my way is clear.
I shall, I will, I must become a knight.

Sigune:

Then do it and meet your ruin!
Behold this dead one! That is you yourself.
Here is the gate that, threatening, opens to you.
And now receive the name that you carry:
"Parzival" did your mother name you crying:
"Midmost through," for he, who has begot you,
pierced her midmost through the heart, so that she sank,
colorless, down upon the dark ground of the world.

Parzival:

Midmost through....

Sigune:

Receive, then, too, the inheritance
of your father; take back the lost crown
of three countries the enemy stole from you:
the crown of Anjou, Waleis, and of Norgals.

Parzival:

Did you know my father?

Sigune:

Child, I knew him. He fell in heathen lands, far
over the sea before Baghdad's white gates.

Parzival:

And left behind no brother or sister for me?

Sigune:

Ah, Herzeleide must have kept this tale
from you, for to her it was bitter as gall.
Hear then: in far distant Moorish lands
Gahmuret took his first wife, beautiful,
and dark was she as night, the Queen of the Moors.
When he left her to see his homeland again
the yearning grew great in her heart
and, like a flower thirsting for the rain,
she closed her sweet petals, and died.
And yet—so I've heard it told—
she bore a single son, strong of limb
and noble in spirit; the skin of his face
and his body is black and white. His name
is Feirifis; his fame streams forth from the lands
of the East like a shining light. This is your brother.

Parzival:

O, that I might see him!

Sigune:

Now you know all. Choose then your lot.

Parzival:

It is chosen.

Sigune:

Then ride forth
and take the stroke that will dub you knight,
the wound from which you'll die.

(*She bends again over the dead man and covers his face with her hair. Parzival begins to ride on.*)

Parzival:

I die? No.
And if I died ten times, I'd still live . . .
Parzival . . . midmost through . . .

(Parzival's encounter with Ither is briefly signified. An image of a great red knight looms. Parzival staggers back, then hurls the light javelin he carries at the image, which falls. Parzival rushes offstage toward it.)

Scene 4 Gurnemanz: "Question Rends the Veil of Secrecy"

Dining Hall in Gurnemanz' Castle

Parzival has just shared a meal with Gurnemanz, his daughter Liase, and a steward of the castle—these last two have just left the table. Parzival is downcast because there has been talk of knighthood, and he realizes his murder of Ither hardly qualified him for that calling.

Parzival steps to the window, through which he looks gloomily down upon the river. During the meal, the evening's light has stolen away, and it begins to grow dark. Pages clear the table and bring in lights.

Gurnemanz (*approaching Parzival, good-naturedly*):

My friend, I have no right to probe the cause
of your unhappiness. Still, you are a puzzle
to the eye, your inward and your outward parts
fitting ill-together. If you trust me,
and would respect your beloved mother's counsel
and take to heart the word of one older than yourself
then do not shut your heart's door to me now.

Parzival:

I trust you, and would like to tell you all.

Gurnemanz:

I thank you. So give me now the right
to several questions.

Parzival:

Ask!

Gurnemanz:

How is that you say
you are no knight? King Ither's knightly vesture
I see upon you, and yet you are not he.

Parzival:

I took it from him.

Gurnemanz:

And did he let you take it?
Did he not defend it, in wild fury?

Parzival:

I killed him.

Gurnemanz:

What?

Parzival:

With the spear,
the light one, that I always used for hunting
I struck him through the eye, and he fell down, dead.

Gurnemanz (*shaken*):

Ither fallen! Ither's blood spilled out
upon the dust of earth. O vengeful fate!

Parzival:

And then I took his weapons, but did not know
how to use them. I took myself
for a knight.

Gurnemanz:

What, so you were not trained
in the use of weapons?

Parzival:

No. I grew up
in the forest, with my mother. In a dream,

there appeared two knights; their light shone
on me. I left my mother to become a knight as well.

Gurnemanz:

And so you met
great Ither, and fought against him, unarmed?

Parzival:

I had only the clothes my mother gave me
which she admonished me never to remove;
then I had, too, my slender spear.

Gurnemanz:

You have felled the strongest in the world
whom Arthur himself could not check, or subdue.
You took his dress, and with that, his very body,
the glowing power of the blood that brought
Ither every victory, and wild renown.
For the colors upon his sword and shield
that purple-red, were no accident:
Ither's blood shot to the edge of his armor.
You took that armor from him; from now on,
you are the Red Knight. Your wild adventuring
has brought you office in this world. Have you
thought well on this, my dear brother?

Parzival:

I wanted the bright armor, and so took it.
I haven't thought about it at all.

Gurnemanz:

So now turn your heart, your spirit,
to your new office. For woe to you, and woe
to everyone if you misuse it!

Parzival:

I ask you, then, to counsel me.

Gurnemanz:

You have the duty now, to become a knight—
more truly so, than Ither himself was.
For Ither carried the robber's saucy heart

within his breast, but you, my friend, must study
humility.

Parzival:
What is humility?

Gurnemanz:
That, no matter how high
you hold your head when riding 'gainst the foe,
you bow it to the One who makes and giveth all.

Parzival:
My mother, too, told me to obey him.

Gurnemanz:
Honor your mother, friend, but now please stop
always speaking of her, like a child.

Parzival:
But I loved her, and the tongue speaks gladly
of whom one loves.

Gurnemanz:
Still, you should stop that tongue
for while the child's soul is left open
as the field, the man locks his feeling
deep in the cave of his bosom.
Your mother's clothes you've worn 'til now.
I asked you to lay these aside, forever.
And yet I still see you wear those old
and clumsy shoes, which will earn you nothing
but disdain. Follow my advice, and take them off, too.

Parzival:
Alas, you distress me. When she gave me them
my mother blessed these shoes with her kiss
and tied the laces, and I have never
untied the bow she knotted then for me.

Gurnemanz:
You should unloose them. For the mother-husk
must crack, as you stretch up toward manhood.

Since you have won the red armor for your own,
you must become *yourself*, newly born
in your own being, and in the depths of God.
Now you must learn knighthood, from the ground up.

Parzival:

So you have hope, sir, that I may lift
myself to knighthood?

Gurnemanz:

If you're one with courage,
you will not fail. And yet it is not fate
nor strength alone that makes a worthy knight.

Parzival:

How should I begin, then?

Gurnemanz:

Let no one who's in need seek your help
in vain. Not for your own sake do you
become a knight; knighthood is service.
Fend off evil, and preserve righteousness,
be subject to women, for the rays of heaven,
caught in the clear cup of their hearts
go wonderfully broken through the world.
Honor each as if he were your brother, nay—
yourself; honor, too, the manhood of your foe
and, in heat of victory, hold pity in your heart
and show mercy to him who asks it of you.
To conquer—yes—yet *not* to kill,
have you chosen the sword and bright lance.
Respect every man's freedom, and do not force
your way into the inner temple of the heart.
Therefore, desist from too much question. Question
rends the veil of secrecy, and he who asks
too often condemns himself to forward thievery.

O friend, o brother, listen to my voice
that urges you to seek the crest of knighthood.
For Arthur will pass—the world that bore him
is vanishing. If there is rescue, it cometh
from the knight of new blood, who, like purple wine,

brims with spirit. If God calls you
to such knighthood, I implore you, brother,
prepare, and make ready all your powers.

Parzival:

Sir, your words glow, and kindle
a fire-brand within my breast!

Gurnemanz:

So let it burn, and shine!

Scene 5 Liase: "All Art is Lost"

In the Castle Garden

In the background, the wall of the castle's chapel. Roses climb the wall. A bench stands off to one side. Liase on the bench. The Castellan enters from the adjacent castle-court.

Liase:

Castellan! Are you returning from the field
where our young friend is schooled in battle?

Castellan:

Indeed.

Liase:

So then, quickly, tell me, how
did he fare?

Castellan:

O, dear child, on him
all art is lost!

Liase:

What? Has he done poorly?
Speak, father! Did he fall from his horse, or....

Castellan:

He was not to be taught.
No sooner had he seen knights ride in joust,
than he sprang up, master of the art.
He rode straight against our most accomplished knights
and, with a single thrust, knocked the proudest
off their saddle.

Liase:

You witnessed this?

Castellan:

This, and more. It was as if lightning
struck in him, when he saw the swords
flash and cross. With sharp eyes, he followed
the whirring light, grasped each thrust and counter.
Then, when his turn came, his lightning blade
shamed our ablest swordsmen.

Liase:

You're telling tales.

Castellan:

Who did not see, could scarce believe it, child.
What is happening here? cried the knights.
What is happening? cried too, Sir Gurnemanz.
The boy must stem from a noble root; knighthood's
in his very blood. But listen! They come.
Greet our brave friend for me! (*leaves*)

Liase:

Did I not guess as much? Not glimpse the hero
in fool's clothing?

(*Gurnemanz and Parzival arrive. They have both put off their armor.*)

Gurnemanz:

Greet your friend, my child, and marvel.
What happened on the battlefield today remains
a mystery; no matter—he is transformed.
Look on him! In body as well as spirit,
a new being; he is now himself.
We must quickly make him into a knight.

Parzival:

I have you to thank for what I am
and will always thank you.

Gurnemanz:

And yet your schooling's not yet ended.
Take him, child, into your confidence
while I rest from our morning's work.
Teach him what only a woman's mouth
can speak of. If he grasps *this* readily as
the sword, we'll not delay fit consecration.

Liase:

I am a maid, father, no woman, yet;
How, then, should I teach him?

Gurnemanz:

Ask your heart!
It will not deny you answer. (*leaves*)

Liase:

Come sit by me! (*Parzival obeys.*)
What should I teach you then?

Parzival:

How one behaves with women, teach me that.

Liase:

My friend, the art is short and long.
One loves them. All's contained in that.
(*Parzival looks at her in puzzled silence.*)
What Love is, my friend, only the heart knows.
For when two hearts are bound together, one dies
wholly into the other, and, dying, both
break through to Life.

Parzival:

As you know this, do you then love?

Liase:

Ah,
you are not supposed to ask, but know.

Parzival:

Oh, dear maid, forgive me that!

Liase:

Now you are wholly mute. What is it?

Parzival:

I am listening.

Liase:

Speak, rather!

Parzival:

Obedient to command, I am silent.

Liase:

If you disdain to speak with words, speak
some other way.

Parzival:

How?

Liase:

How can I teach you
if all appears beyond your grasp?

Parzival:

May I ask you...

Liase:

Ask, for heaven's sake,
before my heart is choked.

Parzival:

You told me of brothers that once were yours
whom a fierce enemy took from you.
Tell me his name, so I may avenge your distress.

Liase:

That's what you wish? You'd still my grief
with the sword?

Parzival:

The enemy—
what is his name? Speak!

Liase:

King Clamide, who killed my brothers like wild beasts,
ignoring their pleas for mercy.

Parzival:

How came it that your brothers took the field
against Clamide?

Liase:

They brought help to Conduiramur,
my father's niece.

Parzival:

Conduiramur?

Liase:

What strikes you so?

Parzival:

Conduiramur? What a wondrous name!
Tell me, what does it mean?

Liase:

Don't ask me this.

Parzival:

Conduiramur.

Liase:

Why are you staring so—

Parzival:

She may be in need
while I sit here, in idle question.

Liase:

Do you want to go to her?

Parzival:

The knightly code demands
defense of those in danger. Can you not
name the place, where I may find her?

Liase:

My father's coming. Ask him.

Parzival:

You turn away from me?

Liase (*vehemently*):

My father! Ask my father!

Parzival:

Have I done something wrong?

Liase:

Let me be! Ask my father!

Gurnemanz (*approaching*):

You are ending, I see. Very well. Liase,
break off some roses and bind them into a wreath
so that we can crown our friend a knight. (*Liase obeys.*)

Parzival:

Who is Conduiramur? Will you tell me, sir?

Gurnemanz:

The beautiful queen of Pelrapeire,
my sister's child. Who told you of her?

Parzival:

Is she in distress?

Gurnemanz:

Clamide's two mighty armies
surround and besiege her city. All my power,
my two son's blooming lives, I gave—in vain—to free her.

Parzival:

I will go to her.

Gurnemanz:

In vain, all in vain.

Parzival:

She must be rescued.

Gurnemanz:

So thought I, for never has a woman
more guiltlessly born the wrath of fate.
But the hand of evil was too strong.

Parzival:

I am called! My heart is clear. I will ride.

Gurnemanz:

Is there nothing that can keep you here?
(*indicating Liase, who comes, head bowed, with the wreath*)

Parzival:

God bless you, for what you've given.
God bless her, too. But I must do
the bidding of my heart.

Gurnemanz (*after a pause*):

Very well, then. Kneel, my friend.
(*draws his sword*)
Thus I dub thee Knight, that you may henceforth
serve the good that called you to the sword.
Crown him, Liase! Be it for triumph,
or for death. (*She does so.*)

Parzival:

You have fulfilled the dream in which first I glimpsed
the sword's bright gleam. Eternal thanks. And now
live well!

Liase (*with inner terror*):

You are going?

Gurnemanz:

To hold him—is in vain. Bid farewell,
my child.

Liase:

My friend, my brother—

Parzival:

God be with you! (*hurries away*)

Liase (*falling upon her father's breast*):

He'll not come back.

Gurnemanz:

His way, like the sword,
leads through the heart of things themselves.

Scene 6 Conduiramur: "Led by Love"

Pelrapeire

Square in front of the royal castle. At the rear of the square are the steps that lead to the entrance to the castle. In the foreground, on the right, is a linden tree. Evening. The square is filled with people of all kinds, all of whom are starved and exhausted (there has been no food in the besieged city for some time), and show signs of despair and longing. Old men are supported, children carried; some people are on barrows, some on biers; even some corpses are set down.

The bells of the nearby church begin to ring.

The People:

Conduiramur! Conduiramur! Beloved queen!

(Conduiramur enters, coming out the gate of the castle towards the rear. She is led by her chief steward, Einhard. She takes a step ahead of Manfiliot and looks, shaken, over the people who stretch out their arms towards her, lift children towards her. Suddenly she falls to her knees and hides her face. All remain silent, overpowered.

At this moment, Parzival arrives at the linden tree. He makes a path for himself through the people and climbs up the steps, stopping half-way up.

Manfiliot makes Conduiramur conscious of Parzival's presence, and she quickly straightens herself. Parzival stands motionless, gazing on her.)

Parzival (*quietly*):
Conduiramur!

Einhard:
My friend, I greet you
in the name of Pelrapeire. Your arrival
was made known to us some time ago. Where
have you been lingering? Be welcome here.

Parzival:
I was in church.

Einhard:
Have the grace, then, to tell
how you passed the armies that surround us
and what has led you to our city.

Parzival:
Your enemy, busy feasting, did not hinder me.
I seek shelter here.

Einhard:
And here you find hunger
and death. If these do not fright our guest,
let me once more bid him welcome. Here stands
the queen. She may provide what you have asked for.

Parzival:
Conduiramur!

Conduiramur:
You call me by my name!
And so, knew me even before our eyes had met.
Since you have not scorned this city of tears,
I embrace you, my most honored guest,
and greet you as brother and as friend.
(*She descends a few steps to him, embraces, and kisses him.*)

The People:
Help, Knight, help save the queen!

Parzival (*ignoring the cry of the people*):
God bless you, gracious mistress!

Conduiramur:
Follow me inside.

The People:
Conduiramur! Conduiramur!

Conduiramur:
(*She turns towards the people, raising her hands heavenward.*)
Heaven be with you all.

The People:
Help the queen! Conduiramur!

In the Castle of Pelrapeire, Parzival's bedchamber

(Parzival asleep upon his bed. On a night table, an extinguished candle, and a small picture of the Virgin Mary. Clearly, though softly, one hears the bells from the church tower ring twelve times, signalling the midnight hour. Conduiramur enters, bearing a candle. She is wrapped in a king's royal purple cloak, a white nightdress underneath. She kneels by Parzival's bed.)

Parzival (*awakens*):
Who's there?
Conduiramur! For heaven's sake, don't kneel
before me; it behooves you to kneel before God
not before mortals. Rise! Stand up!
(*Conduiramur stands.*)

Conduiramur:
I've awakened you. Will you forgive me? O friend,
I've come to you at night's most hidden hour.
I beg of you, do not think ill of me.
I do not seek what the minstrels call love;
I came, driven by my innermost heart, because
I trust in you.

Parzival:

Mistress,
I'll not have you stand, while I lie stretched
comfortably out upon a warm, soft bed.
Please, take this couch, while I linger elsewhere.

Conduiramur:

I'll not chase you from your rest.

Parzival:

Still, I'll not suffer you to stand like a maid
with bare feet by my bed.

Conduiramur:

How else should it be?

Parzival:

Noble mistress, since you say
you've trust in me, lie here by my side.

Conduiramur:

And if I do, say, under what sign
shall this be?

Parzival (*looks around, indicates the image of Mary*):

The sign—of the Virgin.

Conduiramur (*takes off the cloak*):

The purple, I let fall, and am covered
by this shirt's snow alone.

Parzival:

Who are you, lady? You are beside me, and yet
I am alone, wonderfully sheltered in my self.
Do our beings blend? As I talk, it is as if
my soul were speaking with itself.

Conduiramur:

If I am enfolded in you, and you in me
then is my distress yours as well.

Parzival:

Speak,
that I may hear, and salve our single heart.

Conduiramur:

Surrounded by enemies, calling in vain for help—
where may I find rescue? With wild, flaring passion
Clamide desires my body; my land is wasted,
my people starved, and no longer able to withstand
Clamide's fury; tomorrow he'll storm the castle.
For the last time, I rest sheltered by the shield
of night; tomorrow brings shame, or death.

Parzival:

That this shall not be, the God that pours fire
into the blood shall help me. Do not despair,
my lady. Just as the longing to stand by you
sent me here on eagle's wings, so
will I stand before your chaste body
—an angel, now, since God has called me—
and hurl swords of flame upon Clamide's head.

Conduiramur:

Do you believe in victory?

Parzival:

I believe,
that if God sent me, he'll send, too,
the strength to make me equal to the fight.

Conduiramur:

O friend, you
so soothe my teeming soul, that I
shall lay my ahead upon your breast, and seek,
like a child, sleep's tender blessings.

(*She nestles and sleeps.*)

(*In the ensuing darkness, Conduiramur steals away; the bed is removed. Light gradually dawns as the watchman speaks the the following lines. During this dawning, a page helps Parzival arm for battle.*)

Voice of the Watchman:

The hoof of day beats through dark vale.
Look, he ascends in robes of light.
Hark, o true ones, hear my tale;
run, already, is the race of night.

Over the sea rolls the sun's bright wagon;
purple wine pours from out his flagon.
Ye who love, mark me aright:
run, already, is the race of night.

If you'd keep the heart's secrets hidden
from the spreading gaze of day,
do, lovers, as birds are bidden;
rise, and fly away.

Parzival (*alone, fully armed, outside Clamide's tent, his voice powerful and threatening*):

Out, Clamide! I challenge you to battle!
Ho, heraho! Clamide, do you hear me!
Ho heraho! In the noble name
of Conduiramur, I challenge you—

Clamide (*from off-stage, mockingly*):

Ho heraho! You cock! Ho heraho! You donkey!
(*Clamide enters, armed.*)
Has she made a fool of you, too, the sweet lady?
Are you not man enough to scorn the sugar cubes
she lays at your feet? Cry now, you red cock;
when you lie in the dust, you'll cry in vain
for mercy. Come, at it!

(They fight; Clamide falls; Parzival kneeling, spent and penitent, by his fallen foe. Conduiramur enters, dressed in white bridal attire, carrying the royal purple cloak she had worn in Parzival's bedchamber. She lays the mantle across his shoulder, and stands back. Parzival gradually revives, rises, turning away from the dead Clamide to Conduiramur. They kiss and embrace warmly.

Now others enter as the scene is changed into a throne-room in the castle. Clamide is taken off; two simple thrones brought in. A page helps Parzival out of his armor, Conduiramur helps him don the cloak. Einhard, chief steward, and Manfiliot, a hermit, in attendance on Parzival and Conduiramur who sit unostentatiously, side by side, on the two thrones.)

Einhard:

You sit now in higher station than when,
this morning, you left this house. It behooves us
to obey the hero who has rescued our city.
Yet one request we'd make of you—the name,
and noble line of he who now rules us,
our queen's beloved husband, our own king.

Parzival:

That I will gladly say. I am called
Parzival, and my birth, indeed, is noble.
My father, Gahmuret, was king of three realms
and the woman who bore me—o woe!—the world calls
the Lady Herzeleide.

Einhard:

So be greeted, son of the illustrious tribe
from which Arthur himself springs, and to which
the holy office of the sword is given by high heaven.
Born to the sword, today you have splendidly revealed
its shining mission.

Manfiliot:

Yet let me point toward still another truth,
a mystery known only to those who dwell in spirit.
Your mother's line, Parzival, is rooted
in deeper, more secret ground; she stems from the line
of knights that gather round the Holy Grail.
The light of the Grail is hid by a veil
I dare not touch, yet I will say this:
if any were to be worthy of your deepest honor,
it is your mother. Cherish her as a vessel
into which the light and grace of the heavenly
constellations
flow as one.

Conduiramur:

So let us greet you then as one sent to us
by heaven. But what has struck you so—why
look you downcast upon the earth? You are pale...

Parzival:

O let me do what I must! To you,
Einhard, I give over all that is mine—
city, castle, land—so that you may care
for this wounded realm like a good doctor
and, with the patient wisdom that is yours,
restore all to glowing health. But for now
dear friends, leave us, for I long for a word
with my wife, alone. Strength be in your rest!

(*Einhard, Manfiliot exit.*)

Conduiramur:

O Parzival!

Parzival:

My mother never called me
by my name. Would that she had!

Conduiramur:

So let me now fulfill a mother's right.
You are silent? You look at me so wide-eyed
and dumb—

Parzival:

Beloved—

Conduiramur:

You hide a secret from me
that moves you—

Parzival:

That, which hides myself.
I left my mother—ran away. Now,
I am admonished. Three times her name
has sounded like a call. She herself beckons me —

Conduiramur:

Alas!
You'll go from me—

Parzival:

I must seek my mother.
I must tell her, dear one, of the fate
that's befallen me; must lead her to you.

Conduiramur:

You'll go. You'll leave me here, even before
you've wrapped your arms wholly around me.

Parzival:

I shall never leave you. I stream
ever towards you; wherever I wander, I wander always
only in you.

Conduiramur:

But you'll ride. Oh,
and when you ride, destiny will swirl up
round you, because where you are, is destiny.

Parzival:

Let us this night still rest united;
let darkness close over us like a cloak
full of eternity, for eternity is there
where we break into our inmost soul
like an eagle into sunlight. Is this not enough?

Conduiramur:

O Parzival!

Parzival:

When I rode away, my mother
sank down upon the threshold, but I did not
turn back. Now I must return to mend
the cleft I caused, and to ask her about that
which fills my soul with holy shuddering: the Grail.
I will not hide from destiny.

Conduiramur:

I see I cannot hold you here. Alas
this night will be for me both life and death—

Parzival:

Conduiramur—

Conduiramur:

I throw my arms
around your body, that is mine as is my heart,
and bid farewell, now and then and eternally!

ACT II

Scene 7 Amfortas: The Fisher King

Amfortas and two fisherman in a boat on a crystal-clear lake. Amfortas lies half-upright in the boat upon a kind of bed. His dark blue clothing and the cover of the bed are hemmed with gold and decorated with two silver doves. The fishermen likewise wear lilac cloaks. Amfortas' countenance is pale and full of misery. One of the fishermen hauls a silver net on board, the other steers the boat with the tiller at the stern.

Amfortas:

Again nothing? No fish within the net?
The depths that nourish us hold back their treasure.
Otherwise we'd certainly catch a little
for our table. This will not still our hunger.
Alas, the mildness of the moist element
soothes me no more. Saturn once more squares
the sun, frosting my wound. O the agony
that cannot be healed!
Let us go! It is late. We'll catch no more.

Fisherman:

Just this little stretch until the post
on which we tie the net.

Amfortas:

Leave it, my brother!
It is in vain.

Parzival (*comes riding from the wood and stops in wonder*):

Where am I? What wonderful path
plunging ever more deeply into the wilderness
leads me here? A lake in quiet wood
where all the birds are silent, and a stillness,
flowing like crystal, clothes the surrounding rocks
in silver.

Amfortas:

What seek you, Lord?

Parzival:

I am lost—

Amfortas:

Lost? The right path?

Parzival:

The night has fallen—

Amfortas:

The night? The day of the heart.

Parzival:

I seek shelter—

Amfortas:

Shelter? Have you shelter
not within yourself?

Parzival:

A covering roof, a bed—

Amfortas:

Eternity and depth, are those not
roof as well as bed?

Parzival:

What the knight offers
the knight, who comes in late hour.

Amfortas:

Let yourself be told, friend, that within the reach
of thirty miles is nowhere here a house,
be it other than the one I show you.
Raise your glance to that outcropping rock
which, though broad in base, sweeps gently upward.
See the castle at the pinnacle? That
is the place that will shelter you this night.
Climb upwards on the path, fearing neither
the sudden chasm, nor the water's thunderous noise,
and you'll soon reach the place you wish to find.
Knock at the gate, and when someone asks

what you seek, ask admission in the name
of the Great Fisher. Your words will not
be in vain. Above, you will see me again.

Parzival:

Take my thanks,
Great Lord, and remain disposed towards me.

Amfortas:

To the other shore!

Parzival:

The Great Fisher? Lying there in the boat?
Upon his clothes a dove of silver?
Be quiet heart, be still! Here is no room
for question. The path upwards before night falls!

Scene 8 The Grail Castle: Womb of Humanity

Front hall, closed off by a great round arch. It is lighted by two lamps, one on each side. Behind the arch, a huge curtain hangs; it is deep blue, and covered with silver doves.

Parzival is led in by a boy in Grail dress. The chamberlain comes forward to meet him, carrying a purple gown.

Chamberlain:

Welcome, sir, you who have been sent
to bring us fresh joy and hope. Repanse de Schoie,
the pure and queenly maiden, sends you this royal cloak.
Loosing it from her shoulder, she spoke these words:
"Give our worthy guest this purple covering
for that which redeems us from stain and sorrow—
Love—rays forth in its hue's glowing shades.

Parzival:

This comes from the shoulder
of a virgin?

Chamberlain:

Yes, our queen.

Parzival:

I receive it in awe, and without question.

Chamberlain:

So come, the table is prepared for you.

(He strikes a great metal sun-gong. As soon as he does so, the Grail bells begin to ring. The curtain opens. One sees a dinner hall in the inner room. This is round, without pillars, and great arches span the walls. Above the hall, there is a great dome of crystal-like blue-green, upon which the constellations of the zodiac shine.

A line of knights and pages enters, carrying Amfortas upon a bed. Amfortas is clothed in royal purple attire.)

SONG Knights' Chorus

You who bear the suffering of the world,
Wounded by the spear, fallen from above,
Burdened by caprice of wrath and love,
You who bear the lot of us all,
Guilty as we, whose guilt will increase!
Restless as we, who live without peace!
Dying are we, and damned to life,
Always consumed in dying's strife,
Shivering in ice, twisting in fire.
O woe, your shame, your blood, your desire!

Amfortas:

I thank you. The place there, noble guest
is prepared for you. Come and take
what is yours.

(*The Chamberlain leads Parzival to his table.*)

Send for the Grail.

Chamberlain:

You know, noble King,
The Grail does not appear before the lance
has come. *(Amfortas turns away in pain.)*

All:

Woe, woe, the lance!

Amfortas:

The lance comes!

Chamberlain:

Open the portal!

(A column of black-clothed knights appears; the leader carries the lance.)

SONG Song of the Black-clothed Knights

Origin of suffering,
Origin of death,
Poisonous lance,
Brazen thorn—
You who mortally pierce
our tender budding life
again and again—
You, who of wantonly spilled blood
darkly drink,
again and again—
Accept from us, terrible omen,
Our devoted homage,
Our reverent greeting.

(The lance is carried to Amfortas. Amfortas bows his head deeply with a gesture of the greatest, yet inwardly contained, pain. The lance bearer holds the point over his head. Drops of blood fall upon the crown of Amfortas' head.)

Lance-bearer:

Be baptized in blood!
Your own fire
burns your head.
Grasp who you are.

Amfortas:

Woe is me!

All:

Woe to humanity. Woe to the Grail King!

Amfortas:

Is there no one to save me? *(All turn to look at Parzival.)*

Lance-bearer:

There is no one.

Chamberlain:

No one.

All:

No one. *(All the knights hide their faces.)*

Amfortas:

Send for the Grail!

Chamberlain:

The Grail nears!

Amfortas:

Greet it!

(The Grail procession enters the room. Four crowned maidens with two burning lamps lead the way. Then two more with golden footstools, one of which is placed before Amfortas, the other before Parzival. Four more maidens with large candles and four with an eating-board made of hyacinth garnet for Amfortas. Then two princesses with silver knives accompanied by candlebearers. The board is placed before Amfortas, and the knives laid out upon it. Then the 18 women form a group at Amfortas' feet behind the golden table-setting. Now there enter six maidens with burning balsam vessels. Repanse de Schoie follows them; she bears the grail-stone on a green cloth. All of the women are clothed in green cloth. Only Repanse wears a snow-white, gold-embellished gown. As the Grail enters, heavenly light of great clarity and softness spreads over the room. The blue of the dome emerges with special purity. The Grail-bells begin ringing once again; the procession climbs up to Amfortas, goes past him and moves to the lower level on the other side of the room. All the women

move as two groups of twelve each, which leaves room in the middle for Repanse de Schoie. She approaches the table and sets down the Grail.)

SONG Be Greeted Holy Grail

All:

Be greeted, Holy Grail,
Perfection out of paradise!
You who are root and branch in one.
Starry stone of the depths,
The ground of the world made light,
Gift of the heavens and of grace.
You cube and you sphere,
You all and one,
Past and future,
Death and life,
You beginning and end,
You image and truth.

Repanse:

You who ennoble us, when we look upon you,
receive greeting, receive thanks
from the lips you have chosen
to speak these words
of blessing.
You feed my eyes
with noble light,
you nourish my heart
so that I no longer am in want
for bread or for wine.
Praise the mystery
that God reveals before us.
Nature is new-born
the Word, made flesh.
All things whole
in eternity.
Prepare for the meal!

Amfortas:

Reveal the third chamber! Let Titurel see
the radiant loveliness of the Grail!

(The curtain above Amfortas is opened. Behind it, Titurel sits on a throne dressed in a black garment adorned with gold. His face reveals the spiritual transparency of great age. His long, silver-white hair covers his shoulders, his flowing beard, his breast and lap. Supported by two maidens in the same black attire, he rises, and, as if in a gesture of blessing and mercy, raises his arms and sinks into contemplation of the Grail. Amfortas is bowed. His face expresses mute pain.)

Titurel:

Nourish the old one
that he'll not die.
That there be preserved
the divine Word.
Let all touched by time
know the everlasting.
Beginning and End
run together in one.

Amfortas:

Who breaks the spell? *(All but Titurel look at Parzival.)*

Chamberlain:

No one.

Amfortas:

No one.

All:

No one. *(They hide their faces.)*

Amfortas:

Begin the meal!

(The Grail knights rise. Each carries a white cloth in his left hand and a golden goblet in the right. They walk to the Grail and touch the shrine. Then they return to their places with a piece of bread on the cloth and filled goblets.)

SONG Grail Procession

All:

You who bestow the bread
to found the body,
You who bestow the wine
to strengthen the soul,
You who bestow the Light
to illuminate the spirit,

With clarity be seen,
With reverence be honored,
With will be praised,
With goodness, truth, and purity,
O Grail!

(*A page brings Parzival a cloth with bread and a goblet of wine.*)

Chamberlain:

Sir, I invite you to partake. This is the way
of the Grail, which stills every longing
and want of the flesh and gives you strength
for a week's term. Enjoy what is found
by those who are the helpers of humankind.
For in the innermost womb of humanity
a new humanity is founded. See it here.

Parzival:

By your leave, and the bidding of my host.
(*He eats and drinks.*)

Amfortas:

Ended is the meal! Bear away
the Grail! Return it to its place!

(*Repanse lifts the Grail. The procession moves toward the exit.*)

SONG Purity Goes Before Us

Maidens:

Purity goes before us, bearing the Grail,
We follow in rows and sing,
Hallowing the heights and depths of the world

Like a white swan taken to wing.
Light when the heavenly stone is near;
Night descends in its wake.
Trailing behind us, the path we have left
Rushing darkness will soon overtake.

Knights:

The Horn of the Holy turns away from us now.
For a week, we will be most poor,
wandering 'midst darkness in earth's hollow grave
until we see God's light once more.

Amfortas:

The Sword!

(*The Chamberlain hands him a costly sword with a hilt of rubies.*)

Give it to the guest. Recommend it to him.
In heavy battle, it will lend him aid.
It served me well, until the wrath of God
sent the bite of the spear into my loin.
Take it, my guest. It is the highest moment
that calls to you. Leave the bright steel
not within the sheath. Let its fiery gleam
greet the light to which it is kindred.
Take it, and do as your heart bids you.

Parzival (*receives the sword*):

I thank you.

Amfortas:

Who seizes the moment, the final one?

(*All look at Parzival.*)

The Chamberlain:

Master, no one.

Amfortas (*covering his face*):

No one.

Knights (*likewise, covering their faces*):

No one.

Amfortas (*straightening himself*):
It is time, my friend.
The night breaks. We part. Sleep in peace.

Parzival (*rising*):
I thank you, noble host, as much as my heart
has power.

Amfortas:
Thank me? Go with God. He may help you loose
the knots that you yourself do tie. Live well.
Bear me forth!
(*Amfortas, on the bed, is born away; his train follows.*)

Parzival (*watching Amfortas depart*):
Be still, my heart!

Scene 9 Sigune's Curse

Sigune sits under overhanging rocks. In front of her, in a declivity of rock that is like a chest, lies the embalmed body of Shionatulander, wrapped in white. Sigune has turned grey, her face steeped in pain, her figure gaunt; she wears a grey frock. Her gaze fixed upon the face of her dead beloved, she does not notice Parzival.

Parzival:
Sigune!

Sigune:
Sigune—?
What godforsaken man,
speaks my name in this barren wilderness?
Who are you?

Parzival:
Look at me.
Do you not know me?

Sigune:

I know the dead,
not the living. What do you want here?

Parzival:

I am lost.

Sigune:

Where are you coming from?

Parzival:

O woman,
look at me! You must recognize this face.
(*Sigune looks up at him and shakes her head.*)

Sigune:

You look like no one I have known, no.

Parzival:

Then I am not like myself, and only appear
to bear the name you once gave me.

Sigune:

Do not look at me with such vacant eyes.
Go, ride off—this sacred wilderness
hosts no travelers.

Parzival:

Tell me one thing: is there
a castle near?

Sigune:

Yes, Monsalvasch.

Parzival:

I came from there.

Sigune:

You were not there. O no, no one
who saw the marvels that transpire there
speaks, or stares about like you. None who saw
the king stooped with pain that cannot be stilled. . . .

Parzival:
I saw him.

Sigune:
No.

Parzival:
I found the Great Fisher there on the lake;
I bore the queen's purple-red mantle;
the women, bearing candles, drew past me,
and, at last, the light, that streamed over all—

Sigune (*crying out*):
You saw the Grail! I know you. Night
falls from my eyes. You are Parzival.

Parzival:
Am I?

Sigune:
Merciful heaven!
So this child was called to the Grail!
You saw the radiance, the miracle of light,
saw the suffering, humankind's inmost want,
and brought an end to the pain of the afflicted—
O thanks, that the terror of this wound that tore
the whole world is closed....

Parzival:
What are you saying?

Sigune:
Your spirit will have attained the end of ends
if you, O child, performed a single deed:
asked Amfortas the meaning of his great suffering.
Did you fulfill this task?

Parzival:
I did not ask.

Sigune:
Woe! Woe! O awful

searing woe! O unspeakable pain!
O thousandfold fire! All the hopes of mankind,
dashed! Lost the hour, offered only once
to languishing nature! O endless, irredeemable loss!
Now, dead one, we are dead, and all hope
fled and gone.

Parzival:
For heaven's sakes, woman,
tell me, what you are talking about!

Sigune:
Tell you?
You saw Repanse, saw the Holy Grail,
saw the lance drip blood and pain.
What every heart knows, you could not grasp?
Dishonored body, cursed head, be silent!
Every word that you speak, is scandal.

Parzival:
For God's sake, do not rage. I am ready
for every penance.

Sigune:
Penance, yes, do penance,
when all's past and gone. Your penance
won't win a hair of healing. You lost
your head, when you lost your heart. All's in vain,
all foolishness, fool! You can ask me a thousand
questions—
I'll say no more!

Parzival:
Will you cast me
into darkness, into deserted waste?

Sigune:
You yourself
are night, and waste.
(*She turns away and stares fixedly down upon the dead one.*)

Parzival:

I summon you! By God
in Heaven, who is merciful, I implore you
look up! Do not scorn him who asks
for a parting glance. Sigune!

(silence)

Only face
in this wilderness!

(silence)

Woe to them who hear,
and give no answer! Be they God
or human being.

(silence)

Away!

(off into the wilderness)

Scene 10 Gawain: Three Drops of Blood

Woods near Plimözel

The earth is covered with snow. Three drops of blood can be seen in the snow; Parzival, mounted, is staring motionless at them. The fir grove frames the dark and solemn scene.

Parzival:

Stay with me! Leave me not. With head and heart
I surrender to your spell. O White
you lift me wonderfully
out of the shadowy greyness of this vale
and hold me hovering above the spreading world.
Purity! Did I possess you? Did I lose you? O red
blooming in white like a bright rose,
all blossom—and yet more—a thing all made
of glowing light, the enkindled white of snow
the wound of innocence, bleeding from itself.
Who killed you, purest dove? How? Why?
Conduiramur, I see, it is your image!
I am not lost—not cast out, not

stripped of honor, nor thrust coldly forth
into the night. Over the darkness that yawns
all around me, you go as a star,
holding me in the arms of Love where,
like an Angel, I rest in clouds.
Let me be always so, eternally within you,
high above all that dishonors and that shames.
Do not exile me to errant wandering
through the wasteland void of light and grace.
To you, Conduiramur! Into your heavens!
Let me stand in your enchanted air
scorning the lies of the world, so riddled with sorrow!

(*Gawain, unarmed, comes out of the forest.*)

Gawain:

He stands like a thing of stone, his hollow stare
fixed upon the snow. That noble breast
must harbor some deep, unfathomable pain.
He sleeps; well, then, I'll wake him up!—
Hey, Knight, do you hear? Ho! Who are you?

His senses are extinguished, and yet, his red armor
betrays him. He is the one whom I've sought
so long, the one, I must win as friend.
Parzival! Oh! Your name, too, fails to stir you?
(*rides around him observing*)

His eyes aim towards a single target. There
in the snow, red spots, glowing like rubies!
Love's enchantment holds him fettered.
I shall free you, as I am a knight!
(*dismounts, pulls out a handkerchief, and covers the drops of blood*)

Parzival (*sighing*):

O God! (*looks about*)
Where am I? Night is here!
Who curses me? Who casts me out? Why
did the Angels let me fall?

Gawain:

Parzival!

Parzival:

Who calls me?

Gawain:

I, who have sought you for many moons.

Parzival:

Who are you? Tell me—?

Gawain:

King Arthur's nephew, Gawain.

Parzival:

Gawain! You trouble yourself for my sake?

Gawain:

So you'll become my friend. Perhaps some day
you'll honor me, as I honor you.

Parzival:

Honor?

Gawain:

Great hero,
savior and king of beautiful Pelrapeire,
come with me to Arthur. The King himself
wishes to see you sit within his circle.

Parzival:

Is Arthur here?

Gawain:

The King's court is not far from Plimözel.

Parzival:

The King does not hate me? Scorns not the fool
who felled Ither? Invites me to his table?
Is all this true, or do I still dream?

Gawain:

Arthur bears your destiny ever in his mind.
To find you now, is his chief end.

Parzival (*after a pause*):

Gawain, take this hand. And if it trembles
it is my heart, that—still shaken—wavers.
Do not ask why. Lead me to the King.
Let us ride together, side by side!

Scene 11 Kundry's Curse

A gathering of knights and ladies round King Arthur's Round Table

Arthur:

I greet you, strong and noble hero
who, scarce flown from the nest of childhood,
has taught more tested hearts wonder and silence.
Greetings, you whom we have so long yearned to see
so that we might win you as our friend
and member of our company. Welcome here,
welcome into the circle of King Arthur,
esteemed throughout the world. Though Ither's death
has grieved us, you yourself must be the balsam
for that wound. Grant us our request, noble knight;
enter and join us at the Round Table!

Parzival (*arriving onstage*):

Are these words, whose glad ring fills my heart,
reality? How have I deserved such honor,
and such grace?

All:

Welcome, Parzival! Hail to our friend!

Parzival:

O joy, to find myself in such company
surrounded by Love. The abyss that gaped
beneath my feet, closes; the earth grows green.
So then let me be what you have chosen,
gracious King, a knight of the Round Table!

Arthur:

Do me the honor; sit by my side.
And now music! Let our cups be raised!

(The celebration has just begun when Kundry appears in the background, enclosed in dark shadow. Her visage is awful: like that described in her curse of Parzival. The music stumbles to a halt. Kundry gradually begins to come forward, and darkness follows her, casting more and more of the stage in shadow.)

Lady:

Alas, it darkens!

Knight:

There, see the messenger.

Lady:

Who is that?

Knight:

It is Kundry, the bringer of the Grail's curse.
Woe to him, whom she comes to counsel!

Kundry:

I bring you woe, O Arthur of Bertane,
that you would so dishonor your Round Table.
Why do you invite a poisonous worm to your feast—
one who eats the core of your trees' splendid fruit?
For know: this is the evil art of poison
that whatever its seething force invades—
it will devour like the hungry fire,
not resting, till all around it is destroyed.
You keep company with wickedness
and so this judgment falls upon *your* head.

Arthur:

Though you bring darkness, dread herald, speak
less darkly. Whom do you accuse? Here
are virtue's own. If there be one that prepares
shame for the Round Table, then name him!

Kundry:

His name—is Parzival!

All (*shocked*):
What, Parzival!

Kundry:
To you I offer curse and shame
heartless man, robbed of all true sense!
Called to the highest peak of humankind
you have forfeited the world's redemption
annihilated the last hope of your brother,
and broken the last staff of the blind.
To you the inmost suffering of the soul
did show itself, burning; the pained gaze
did meet your own, pleading and beseeching.
But you kept silent, fool, and did not ask.

Past you went the admonishing spear;
the wound of humankind poured forth black blood;
sighs paralyzed the holy hall—
but you kept silent, fool, and did not ask.

To you the Grail opened up the wonder
of its fullness; the veil of heaven lifted;
amazed, you saw the light pour itself out
furnishing the pure, the eternal feast
but you kept silent, fool, and did not ask.

On you the host bestowed as honoring gift
the holy sword that fashions miracles,
exhorting you to use its cutting edge
to win well-being for the suffering world,
to seize the moment, and rule —
But you kept silent, fool, and did not ask.

Therefore, be cursed! Curse your blind eye,
curse your ear that registers no sound,
curse your heart, that empty yawning hole
of darkness, where no understanding lives.
Your glance is falsehood. Here, then, are your signs!

If you would see your image, gaze at me!
The gaping wolf's maw splits your face for you;
the boar's tooth bares itself protrudingly;

the look of horror stares from unseeing holes;
daggers fortify your clumsy hands
so that you kill whenever you caress.
Loathsome head, your tongue dries up
within your mouth and sprays forth dusty ashes.
A dead man, you bring death to everyone,
even as, through you, the world lost redemption.
Nevermore shall your own heart be healed!
(*Kundry departs. A long shocked silence ensues.*)

Lady:

Woe to our friend.

Knight:

Woe to us all!

Lady:

O Parzival, how has this happened to you?
Speak, noble friend, explain to us
this mystery.

(*Parzival keeps silent, and hides his head. He remains thus, motionless.*)

Arthur:

Friends, let us leave him to his heart.
Whom the hand of the invisible strikes,
we seek in vain to comfort. Whatever we might say,
our words will not serve him, for in the face
of his great pain, all else is smoke. God help him,
even as He has struck him down.
(*All but Gawain leave Parzival.*)

Gawain:

My friend, my brother—I will not leave you.
Your life is my own. Speak, if you can,
for your silence is terrible.

Parzival:

Leave me alone!

Gawain:

To me, that would mean

leaving you to death. Never will I
leave you alone. For you and I are one.

Parzival:

My lot is cast. Heaven itself has judged me.
My presence is the breath of pestilence
to the pure. Let me go!

Gawain:

You must turn again towards the Grail.

Parzival:

Me, to the Grail? Hah!

Gawain:

You must stretch your heart towards it.

Parzival:

My heart? Where is my heart? It is finished.

Gawain:

What will you do?

Parzival:

Ride.

Gawain:

And where?

Parzival:

Where?
To the edge of the world, where no voice sounds,
and no human habitation stands.

Gawain:

O friend, you must save yourself.

Parzival:

Save myself? What a foolish thought.

Gawain:

Then I will do for you

what you refuse to do for your redemption.
Your destiny I shall take, with hope, into my heart.

Parzival:

With hope?

Gawain:

Trusting in the highest God.

Parzival:

Woe! Who is God? You imagine him
merciful, because the human heart cries out
for mercy. But I have come to know him.
My heart burned to do him purest service;
He lifted the staff of the world
and struck me down into the pit of night.
Mercy? All around, the world lies steeped
in pain, in blood, in shame; it groans aloud
and sweetly names this monstrousness—its Father.
Curse you, Tyrant! You whose feet tread with scorn
upon the world you yourself have made.
The wild heart of man's not made
to be the plaything of your changeful moods.
I shall withstand you. To your face, I now
renounce your service, and declare myself free
from every commandment that you, since time began,
have forced upon the race of humankind.
Go your way, and I will go mine also
and between us, let the cleft Earth's abyss yawn.

(*rides off*)

Gawain (*vainly*):

Wait!

ACT III

Scene 12 Sigune: "If you would know the way"

A lonely, nearly impassible forest. Under a cliff a shelter built from newly hewn trees. Parzival forges a path through thick, high brush.

Parzival:

Halt, loyal steed. Man is not so true
as you, and God is as false
as he.... but how is it that I use
that name, which I have not spoken for many years?
Are you not yet extinguished from memory?

Silence, Parzival! Do not speak to him,
for scorn itself is honor. Do not offer it.
He is no more. Do not stand again
in your sepulchre, dead one! For I
am the crypt; and the corpse within—is you.
And over corpse and coffin, the blank sky
broods endlessly in senseless space.
Yes, senseless. For all I do and fight for,
and where I guide my horse day after day
matters not at all. How many years
have I passed on this journey? I do not know.
I press mutely on in a world without sign.
There is no aim, no end. So welcome,
wilderness. This is my place. Who here thinks
of time? Of life, and death? Of Heaven, or of Hell?

But look, even this place is poisoned.
A pale monk has already crept here,
and built himself a hut, where he reads
the psalter of his false God.

Stop, monk, this wood is mine.
(*He dismounts, fastens his horse, and steps up to the hut.*)
Hello, monk, come out!

Sigune:
Who calls me?

Parzival:
A nun! O deluded woman! I wish to see you.
Have you no door to your house?

Sigune:
No.

Parzival:
You live in a cloister?

Sigune:
Yes.

Parzival:
And do not die from hunger?

Sigune:
I am fed by the Grail.

Parzival (*as if struck by lightning*):
The Grail? Where is the Grail?

Sigune:
You are near it. In the veil of these woods,
Monsalvasch lies hidden.

Parzival:
Nun, come to the window,
so we can speak more freely.

Sigune:
I am here. What do you want?

Parzival:
Nothing. But no—can I reach the Grail?

Sigune:
You cannot.

Parzival:

How does it approach
to feed you?

Sigune:

Every Saturday, one of the Grail-company
rides from the castle in the dark of night—
Kundry!

Parzival:

The dreadful one!

Sigune:

The gentle one,
who generously brings me the Grail's holy food.

Parzival:

Who are you?

Sigune:

I am a bride, though my groom lies dead.
Here, sepulchred under the rocks, sleeps
my beloved.

Parzival:

You are Sigune.

Sigune:

Do you know me?

Parzival:

As you must know me. Your curse
lies on me still.

Sigune:

My curse? I curse no one.

Parzival:

Look me in the face!

Sigune:

Parzival!

Parzival:

It is I. And yet, not so, for I
am not myself. Your curse broke my heart
and Kundry swung the scourge over my head.

Sigune:

Anguished soul!

Parzival:

I do not want your pity.

Sigune:

My friend, I cursed you once; now I curse
no one. I pray, pray.

Parzival:

And this gives you peace?

(*She indicates assent.*)

Sigune:

Parzival, how can you go in arms today!?

Parzival:

Today? What is today?

Sigune:

Surely, there is no one in Christendom
who does not know Good Friday.

Parzival:

Time is lost to me.
I no longer count the days; the months,
the years roll past renewing themselves in dream.
I no longer ask the year, or season.

Sigune:

So you despise the sun?

Parzival:

What?

Sigune:

The day, the week,
that unfolds the days of passion
that witnessed the redemption of the world.
Do you not observe it?

Parzival:

The redemption? What is
redemption? There is no rescue!

Sigune:

O lost one,
my beloved, locked in his stony crypt, sleeps
less deep than you; his body only is given o'er
not his soul. Parzival, see it: you are dead!

Parzival:

Dead? Do not these lips move? Warm blood
runs in my veins.

Sigune:

No, cousin, colder
than the snow. No one knows the face
of death as well as I; I see his visage
shadowing your features. Look! your lips
breathe icy scorn upon the spring of life.
O lost one! Do not storm at God!

Parzival:

I fought in his name. He cast me out....

Sigune:

Be still! You know not what your wild words deny.
Hear me, if you would know the way. There,
at your feet you'll discern a path, faint,
yet clearly etched upon the snow. Take it,
and ride to a cave, a hermitage of stone not far
from here, and there you'll find the holy place
where Trevrizent dwells. His spirit, like an eagle,
hovers above this world; peace dwells with him,
and love. Go, discover yourself to him,
and he will give you healing counsel.

Parzival:

A man
of God!? . . .

Sigune:

Your teacher. Now
bow your head, so I may break the seal
of darkness still stamped upon your brow; for these—
—my lips—have known the love that knows
and passes death.

(*kisses Parzival on the forehead*)

Now go!

(*Sigune and her hut disappear, leaving Parzival in the dim shadows.*)

Parzival:

My soul is kindled—glows. Love,
is that you? Flow, tears, flow—
to me you are as mild as spring rain.

Scene 13 Trevrizent: Good Friday's Teaching

The hermit's cave is cut out of rock. In the middle there is an altar-table with a covered cross. To the side, in a niche, a coal fire that lights the room. In the corner, a bed of moss and straw.

Trevrizent (*rises*):

Who knocks? Is someone there?

Parzival (*from outside*):

A stranger, Father.

Trevrizent:

Enter!

Parzival (*enters*):

I thank you.

Trevrizent:

Armed today? Do you not know what day
it is? The great holy day of sorrow?
Take off your weapons.

Parzival:

I will do so gladly.

Trevrizent:

What do you wish? Shelter
I can give you, but food
I do not have.

Parzival:

I seek counsel, Father.
I am fallen into the net of doubt,
and my strength languishes.

Trevrizent:

Sit down.
I will give you counsel, if I can.
What fails you?

Parzival:

Everything, Father.
I ride in darkness, without aim or end.
I hated God; I hate him now and always.

Trevrizent:

What are you saying?

Parzival:

He plunged me in a sea
of shame, and heaped cold mountains of curse
upon my heart. How did I deserve
the chisel of scorn he drove against my naked
breast?

Trevrizent:

Alas, thus speak those who condemn themselves,
the executioners of their own heart. Sir,
disarm yourself before God, for with arms

you can force nothing. God is an inner fire
that can melt the metal from off your limbs.
Who stands against God, stands against himself
and when he fights, aims the blow at his own
midmost part.

Parzival:

So should I be nothing?

Trevrizent:

Nothing of pride
or illusion, for in this nothing,
God's fullness dawns.

Parzival:

Do not tell a knight to learn this lesson!

Trevrizent:

Here hides the riddle of the human being.
Fail to grasp it, and your ship will list
and sink, and you can grasp it only
if you put the armor from off your heart.
For more than bravery, more than courage
is humility; to this, pledge life and being.

So now tell me, Sir, who are you?
Whence do you come?

Parzival:

I come from Anjou. My father
was Gahmuret, who died in heathen lands.
And my mother's name is—Herzeleide.

Trevrizent:

What, you are Parzival? Unblessed child
you left your mother, and broke her heart:
she sank down on the threshold you had crossed,
and, sighing, died.

Parzival:

O God, what are you saying—no!
It cannot be!

Trevrizent:

My sister gave up her life like a dove
met by an arrow.

Parzival:

Your sister! God! You are my uncle!

Trevrizent:

In truth, I am.

Parzival:

O mother, mother, woe! (*He hides his face.*)

Trevrizent:

You weep? God help you.

Parzival (*after a long silence*):

Mother, I speak, and you do not hear;
my eyes search for you, and your eyes
do not meet their gaze; I hurry towards
the chamber you made and kept for me
to embrace you, to throw my arms around your knees
and find it empty. The song you sang to me
vanishes in the forest air. Moon, Moon
of Konvoleis, your gentle visage bleeds—
and I have done it! (*hides his face again*)

Trevrizent (*approaching Parzival once again*):

To bear misfortune that comes
to us from outside, is hard, but the burden
of our own guilt, far greater. Yet still
it must be born.

Parzival:

O Father,
I am guilty of yet another life!

Trevrizent:

Speak.

Parzival:

I killed King Ither, shot him like a beast
in the wood, and stole his armor before
his blood was cold.

Trevrizent:

Woe, brother, woe—he whom you felled
was one of your own blood.

Parzival:

O, I—
murderer of myself!
I shudder to think on all I've done.

Trevrizent:

If you were struck down, was it not
by your own hand? Lucifer's proud hell
abides within our breast. Yet there is, too,
a place, where the tent of God is raised. This place
is deep within; yet he who digs through to it
is redeemed.

Parzival:

Redeemed? Is there redemption for the blasphemer?

Trevrizent:

God's mercy knows no bounds, and yet
is not lightly given. You must die
to your old self, and then—from the blind
night, reach for God's hand once more,
and so, rise new, my son, new.

Parzival (*gripped*):

New! O heart,
that you may be made new!

Trevrizent:

Do you glimpse now what God gave
to this heavy earth? Love.
For God is Love. And it is the light
of Love that shines forth from the Holy Grail.

Parzival:

Speak to me of the Grail!

Trevrizent:

It is a pure stone,
circular and square, clear and shining as day.
Before the beginning, the Grail was; unborn
came it from God's hand, its name inscribed
in the constellations. Angels bore it, hovering
over the earth, and each hour that received it
was stretched into eternity. For know: the heart
of the Earth, its model and its end, is the Grail—
the light of matter, eternal renewal
flowing from the fount of everlasting being.
And know, too: the Earth is humanity,
and so is the Grail the origin of man,
its transfiguring light, his destiny as well.

Parzival:

O, that I had grasped this!

Trevrizent:

Good Friday is the beginning of the world,
the seed of heaven sewn in the dark womb of Earth;
our task is to receive it in our human hearts,
the rocky soil that is the ground of new being.

And, nephew, know—you yourself
are descended from the family of the Grail.

Parzival (*shocked*):

I?

Trevrizent:

You! My brother is Amfortas,
Guardian of the Grail, and its King;
he is uncle to you, the brother of your mother.

Parzival:

O God!

Trevrizent:

The purest lady,
Repanse, bears in her hands
the Grail that consumes each one who is unworthy.

And she, Repanse, the sister of your mother,
is as close to you as I.

Parzival:
Your fiery glance sends a blow
upon my guilty head.

Trevrizent:
Forget yourself!
For look—another of your line bears
a still greater pain. It is Amfortas,
whose life is agony.

Parzival:
Tell me of him!

Trevrizent:
The Grail was given first
into the hands of Titurel, who dwells still
in the Grail Castle. Yet when he—still aglow
with spirit—became too weak to serve, Frimutel
inherited the service. He was slain
in knightly battle, and the Grail-crown
passed to Amfortas. Yet Amfortas fell.

Parzival:
He fell? Fell from grace? How?

Trevrizent:
A woman took his heart;
to him, she was the fairest in the world, and yet,
she was unworthy. For her sake, Amfortas
rode out in quest of love, yet in battle
with a heathen, was wounded in the groin
by a poisonous spear. The wound healed not,
whatever we might do, for whenever one
of the heavens' wandering stars moved
into opposition with the sun, the pain
mounted with renewed force. And so,
suffering ever and again a new hue
of wretchedness, Amfortas lives in restless agony.

Parzival:

O what bitter repentance!

Trevrizent:

And yet still more bitter, the regret, the knowledge
that he is guilty of the crime of which
the wound is but sign—and yet, must still perform
his holy office, appear before the light
pure as the sun. O only the guilty
can measure such pain!

Parzival:

O say, my Father, why is this so?
Why such light, and such great suffering?

Trevrizent:

It is the image of humanity.
We all bear one guilt, and our misdeed
festers, and erupts in pestilential wounds.
We have betrayed God. Amfortas does not bear
the burden of his shame for himself alone;
but for us, as well. Called, as we are,
to the kingdom of a new and pure life,
we can only wear the crown of our state
upon our head, while languishing in pain.
The Grail sustains us—and yet our wound
heals not.

Parzival:

Father, redemption for Amfortas—will this
not come?

Trevrizent:

If so, it must come from humankind.
Never could God alone redeem our state.
We must grasp what is offered, cup our hands
and drink of the ever-flowing fount of compassion.
When the heart feels the suffering of others,
and the will is driven to help, even to the limit of
self-sacrifice; when one's whole being burns with the
question:
why is this? what can I do? Then, by the Grace of God,
redemption may come to us in our need.

Parzival:

O, what pain fills me, and what fire!
Am I Amfortas then? The spear pierced me.

Trevrizent:

Once the Grail announced in holy script
that a knight would come to Monsalvasch
to bring about this healing with a question.
The knight did come; alas, he did not ask!
A fool he was, not knowing even himself;
he let Amfortas suffer, let the Grail
spend its grace, saying nothing. They
cast him out, and he was no more seen.

Parzival:

No more seen.

Trevrizent:

With him was lost the healing
of all humankind.

Parzival:

And as the curse
befell him, he scornfully turned his back
on Heaven, and became a fiend to God.
Do you know him?

Trevrizent:

Brother, do I hear aright? You?

Parzival:

I. Lost and disappeared am I
before God and man, my light
is darkness; fallen to rubble is my house
and can no longer be rebuilt again. (*falls to his knees*)

Trevrizent:

Beloved nephew, God is a sea; with what misdeed
can you exhaust the goodness of that ocean?
One thing is promised you: the light of freedom.
You may use it as you will. If you tear

yourself from God's heart, He'll not stop you,
but you will ride on towards your destruction.
Yet whatever you have done, if you turn back
He will receive you, as He received the son
that was lost and returned to him, starving—
with a heart more glowing than all the Angels.
Let go all that has so gripped you,
even the hate and rage against yourself.
Accept your guilt as a crown of thorns
that festively is pressed into your brow—
as a spear, that opens up your side,
as a tree, on which you, stretched out,
suffer your own being, unable to tear
yourself away from the fire that burns you.
Desire nothing more than to be formed
as a pure tone by the hand of God,
a still dark tone, becoming a vessel of grace.

(*A host of Angels appears, surrounding Parzival and singing.*)

SONG Accept Your Guilt

Accept your guilt as like a crown of thorns
that festively is pressed into your brow—
as a spear, that opens up your side,
as a tree, on which you, stretched out,
suffer your own being, unable to tear
yourself away from the fire that burns you.
Desire nothing more than to be formed
as a pure tone by the hand of God,
a still, dark tone, becoming a vessel of grace.

Parzival:

Father, I am dead. Pray that God
will make me live again. I thought I
could do all, and look, I could do nothing.
And yet I know: I am eternally
anchored in Him, my name inscribed
in his Book of Love, and truly it cannot
be erased, except by my own hand. I plunge
into a night that is the mother of all nights,

a sea without beginning or end, the womb
of the world.
(*He sinks to Trevrizent's feet and falls into sleep.*)

Trevrizent:
Blessed pilgrim, gliding over the sea
in the breath-light boat of your spirit,
do you feel the void's powerful fullness near?
Is the mysterious midnight sun, the light
that never leaves, rising in you now?
Do not fear: I am. Do not fear!

The Angel choir:

SONG Blessed Pilgrim

Blessed pilgrim, gliding over the sea
in the breath-light boat of your spirit,
do you feel the void's powerful fullness near?
Is the mysterious midnight sun, the light
that never leaves, rising in you now?
Do not fear: I am. Do not fear!

(*The host of Angels disappears.*)

Trevrizent:
The great strong hero becomes a child.
Look: he sleeps in the lap of softest light.
And so the hour of new birth nears.

Scene 14 Feirifis: From the Realm of Dawn

A forest clearing

A fine, dense veil conceals the background. Early morning. Parzival, whose steed stands tied, kneels in profile.

Parzival:

I sail like a ship with heavy freight
in dense grey fog, the near shore only marking
the way behind me and the course before
veiled in obscurity, sinking fast from sight.
For now, stay quiet, heart, and bend more deeply
towards the ground of things.

Yet, look. In the twilight fine cloud fills
and forms a circle, imaging a crown
of silken white, light streaming from within—
O, it reminds me of the Grail, for such pure light
poured forth from it! Yet look, there grows
from the ground, dense and grey, a cube
as if of stone, an altar, and now in the chalice
a white roundness glows with gentle radiance.
The Grail—it is! I see it as if in twilight;
the veil falls from it—fading, the wonder vanishes
into the depths; my senses sink to earth. (*hides his face*)

(*The veil parts and tears open more and more. One becomes aware of the more distant landscape, which rises to the Sea. In a cove, a great number of ships. Feirifis upon a strong steed, in heavy armor set with gems, rides up and halts across from Parzival, in the foreground. Parzival does not notice him.*)

Feirifis:

If I err not, this is the land of evening
towards which I've striven. Thank the almighty
Ahura Mazdah, who has steered my keel
and let me reach this distant goal! Praised
be the holy power of his sunlit head, for here
I'll find my father. Yet who kneels there
on the ground, fully armed, his proud head
so deeply bowed? Are you, O mute hero,
the Guardian of the West? Then I shall
raise you, for I desire entry. This calls
for battle. Stand up!

Parzival:

Who calls me?

Feirifis:
    A stranger. I challenge you!

Parzival:
    Is it a woman
    for whom you fight?

Feirifis:
    No, for Ahura I draw
    my silver sword.

Parzival:
    Sir, him I do not know.

Feirifis:
    So feel his force upon your body!
    For whom do you fight?

Parzival:
    I stand for the Grail.

Feirifis:
    Who is the Grail?

Parzival:
    A God and, too, a human being.

Feirifis:
    This seems strange to me. But enough of words!
    Let us each prepare for battle.

Feirifis (*kneels down and raises his sword*):
    I call upon you, great light of the Sun,
    you fire of all things, all-conquering light.
    You light of my head, my eyes, my limbs,
    you, light of my flashing sword.
    You, be with me! Let your fire strike down
    him who dares resist me, in arms.

Parzival (*kneeling down and raising his sword*):
    I call on you, lightfilled Holy Grail,
    beginning of all the world, and its end.

You magnificent light, you make immortal those
who trust in you. Consume the death in me;
accept him whom you once called as your suppliant.
I do not ask for victory; I plead that your will
shall be fulfilled.

Feirifis:

Are you ready?

Parzival:

I am.

Feirifis:

As am I!

(*They fight. At first the opponents show themselves equally matched. Then Parzival's fighting strength begins to fail.*)

Feirifis (*pressing Parzival back hard with several thrusts*):

Tabronit!

Parzival (*rallying himself*):

Pelrapeire!

Feirifis (*with a blow that brings Parzival to his knees*):

Secundilla!

Parzival (*rising up and striking a blow that brings Feirifis to his knees*):

Conduiramur!

Feirifis (*rising and striking a blow that knocks Parzival down*):

By the Ecidemon!

Parzival (*struggling to his feet and rallying for a deathblow*):

By the Holy Grail!

(*Feirifis crumples; Parzival's sword breaks.*)

Feirifis (*half-upright*):

I live yet.

(*sees Parzival standing as if frozen with broken sword, and, still reeling; stands*)

I stand! Weaponless, you are Death's.

Parzival:

God gave me to him. Thrust home!

Feirifis:

And so shame myself! Never! None
shall avail himself of the splendor of the sword
since yours has abandoned you.
(*throws his sword far from himself*)
We stand equal.

Parzival:

Give rest!

Feirifis:

Gladly. For as long as we rest, we can be friends.
Sit by me.

Parzival:

I do so, and honor you.
For truly, never have I met a champion
equal to you in strength or kingly stature.
Your dress, covered with precious gems
sparkling—like heaven—in a thousand rays
possesses the silent force of the firmament
and there the little snake upon the peak
crowning your helmet with its golden glow
seemed to me to shine in special splendor
as you struck those strong sword-blows
that none I have ever met has struck before.

Feirifis:

My dress, o champion, is truly a tent
of stars, and my limbs infused
with their silent splendor and power
so that none, opposing me, might withstand
my heavy blows, none, 'til this very hour.
But the golden snake upon the crown
is the seed and essence of all powers.
The Ecidemon it is, the holy animal.

Parzival:

My sword has wounded it, and made it bleed.

Feirifis:

And so it broke. Yet truly, remained holy—
for I was struck down.

Parzival:

Even so, God gave me o'er to your will
and put the balance of my life into your hands.

Feirifis:

Should I then kill the one who laid me low
and was the victor? This unashamed hand
stain with murder? So would I condemn myself.
Your sword betrayed you—never yet, your arm.
You are the greatest not only of the West,
but stand before me, ruler of the world.
For know: I am envoy of the East
who lends the essence of its power to me.
I come with the power of the Ecidemon
to vie with the Grail, for whom you fight.
So speak, mighty one: of what race are you,
what is your name, your people, and your realm?

Parzival:

Even if my life is given to you as bond
my name is more to me than life itself.
In freedom can I gladly share it with you
yet never give it you at point of sword.

Feirifis:

There is no force between us, but free will.
And so that you will know this, I will name
my own self first: I am from Anjou.

Parzival:

From Anjou? Impossible. Sir, how can this be?
There is one Lord of Anjou, and I am he.
Who could have wrested from me my father's realm?
Truth cannot be upon your lips, unless you be
the one of whom Sigune spoke, the one dark Belacane
bore in the desert land of palms. If I could see
your face for a moment only, I would know all
I need to know.

Feirifis:

And what was told you, hero,
of my countenance?

Parzival:

Like a written page,
the hues of black and white are shown there, mixed.

Feirifis:

I am he. Look here! (*opens his visor*)

Parzival:

My brother! O my brother!
My Feirifis!

Feirifis:

But what do I call you?

Parzival:

Parzival!

Feirifis:

Parzival!
O great God in Heaven,
you who with your left hand created the realm
of dawn, and with the right, the spreading lands
of evening, where the bright sun seeks its rest—
say, are these not both brothers, since they
are born of one and the same father, to whom
East and West both give themselves as bride?
My brother Parzival, I must not strike you down,
but may love you.

Parzival:

Be welcomed by me, you noble, long-sought for one!
Be received here, into my inmost heart!
When others took joy in their dear siblings, I
was left alone; though my soul oft urged my hands
to stretch in prayer and yearning towards the East.
And now—you are come to me, from there.

Feirifis:

The East looks on me as on the brightest
in its starry host. It fitted me out
with five and twenty ships; I crossed the sea;
came here, to seek my father.
Tell me where he is, so I may greet him.

Parzival:

He who was our father, Feirifis, he is
no more.

Feirifis:

I'll not see him?

Parzival:

As little as I myself
have ever seen him. For before my mother
bore me in pain, he was lost to us in battle.

Feirifis:

Woe to me! And yet am I blessed, for finding you,
you who are my brother and friend and father.

Parzival:

You laugh and cry? As through the flood of rain
the sun will break, so through your great pain
the light of joy streams forth. Yet say, she who bore you,
the fair, dark queen, how is it with her?

Feirifis:

A more tender woman
this world has never seen. She yearned always
for Gahmuret, the Lord who had left her, and lost
her strength and shimmer like the waning moon
and so died.

Parzival:

Like Herzeleide died,
the one who bore me. (*He hides his face.*)

Feirifis:

This fatal, holy yearning, O Parzival, let it bond us, too.
Let us swear an oath of loyalty and love!

Parzival:

Let us swear, brother Feirifis!

Feirifis:

My brother Parzival.

Parzival:

Never will I leave you!

Feirifis:

I hold with you forever.
No longer are we enemies. So can I
reveal to you my holy mystery.
I brought it here so that its wondrous power
might illumine, triumphantly, the great West.
See now this creature, the Ecidemon
the image of all human consummation.
There is a tree called the tree of death;
it rises in you, rises through all the spheres
of the cosmos, and all who live and there exist
stand fastened to its unmoving trunk.
At the foot of this tree, enfolded
in deep and sacred sleep, rests the serpent.
The day will come when your inner heart
calls, and awakens it to divine calling.
Then in you it will open its pure blossoms,
the rays of heaven, whose seeds are everlasting,
and released from petaled fragrance, the Ecidemon
climbs in wondrous circles to the edge of all,
its radiant light consuming all that is stained
by death and decay. The serpent then becomes
a bride, knowledge glittering like gold in her eternal eyes,
while in the flower, the Lord of the world
stands erect, reaching forth his hand
to join his bride in heavenly wedding.
Then vanishes all that was and is and will be,
and that which is ground of all, and without void
breaks through to being. This is the Ecidemon,
at which your sword struck. Preserve this Word,
until it turns to truth within your blood!
Preserve it in deep silence, for understanding
is reserved for those touched by its power.

Parzival:

I accept this gift, so wrapped in mystery;
and will honor the secret in silence until
its truth opens to me.

Feirifis:

Since I have surrendered my highest
secret to you, brother; make known to me,
as well, the holy mystery of the West.
What is the Grail?

Parzival:

A secret, greater still
than that you have shared with me, O Brother.
No human mouth can make it manifest.
Therefore, although you ask, I stand here, dumb.
From the Grail itself you must seek your answer.
For know: though you name me the strongest on Earth,
I myself am unworthy to approach the Grail.
You sink in distress? There is a spring that wells
from the ground of God and is called Grace.
If its water moistens us, all will be revealed
to our best sense. Therefore, let us endure!

Feirifis:

It befits me, brother,
to honor the Word which you have spoken.

Parzival:

Accompany me to a place
where you will witness a mystery that stems
too, from the Grail. For the guardian of the Grail
gave me this sword, that, wiser than its master,
broke upon your head, recognizing the brother
that came from the East. The first blow (so
it was once foretold me) the sword would sustain;
at the second, shatter; but if made whole again,
would never more splinter or be harmed.
Follow me to the smithy, where it will be new-forged.

Feirifis:

You will I follow, dear brother, as half
of my own heart, wherever your strong love
may lead us on.

Scene 15 Trebuchet: The Blacksmith's Forge

Trebuchet's forge in a rocky cave

A niche has been made in one of the cave's stone walls, and a chimney leads from it to the open air. In the niche there burns the forge fire. A powerful bellows hangs on the wall next to it; nearby, the anvil, and various forge tools. In the background, to the right, a spring flows out of the darkness of a rocky overhang and collects in a stony fountain-basin, from there flowing off to the side.

Parzival and Feirifis enter. Trebuchet is hammering at the forge fire.

Trebuchet:

Swing of the arm, hammer blow!
Day and night red embers glow,
So day and night are one.
No ray of sun can enter here
Nor does the silver moon shine where
My deep work is done.

Swing of the arm, hammer blow!
Forging weapons in the fiery glow,
Weapons that will not rust.
Swords that no blow will break,
Shields whose iron band can take
Falsehood's sharpest thrust.

Swing of the arm, hammer blow!
Those who reap the seeds I sow—
The Knighthood of the Grail.
Wielding the flashing sword,
So the dominion of the Word
Will not fail.

Parzival:

Master, let your hammer rest and look
what we bring to you. This strong sword
broke on the shining helmet of this hero.
You made the sword; can you forge it anew?

Trebuchet:

Who are you?

Parzival:

Parzival.

Trebuchet:

Oh, your destiny
is known to me. Give me the proud ruin.
And him?

Parzival:

Feirifis, from the East.

Trebuchet:

Gahmuret's son? I know well
the tale of Belacane's joy and sorrow.
You carry on your helmet the Ecidemon,
full of holy power, an unheard-of wonder.

Feirifis:

How strange, that all this is known to you!

Trebuchet:

I am a man of the cave, and of fire.
I know iron, and the holy word.
The book of man is not closed to me.

Feirifis:

Did you ever feel Ecidemon's power?

Trebuchet:

The serpent bears knowledge.
And yet the snake still lacks
the dove. For intellect is nought without
innocence, and purity of heart. The head

must turn to heart, and the heart, to head.
Do you know the dove?

Feirifis:
No.

Trebuchet:
It is the Grail's, like this sword.

Feirifis:
So show me the Grail!

Trebuchet:
I cannot. Yet one thing I know:
He who knows surrender, who gives himself
as sacrifice: to him, the Grail is revealed.

Feirifis:
So tell me, then, how this might be done?

Trebuchet:
Give me the Ecidemon!

Feirifis:
My power, my light
my deepest secret?

Trebuchet:
If you try to keep it,
you will lose it.

Feirifis:
So, weaponless and naked
I should deliver myself into the hand
of the foe?

Trebuchet:
Like him who enkindled the Grail.

Feirifis:
Mazdah called me to battle. Should I now
renounce all might?

Trebuchet:

Yes, and wholly so.
For one power rules above all others: Love.

Feirifis:

Take it! *(He breaks the Ecidemon from his helmet, and gives it to Trebuchet.)*

Trebuchet:

You are a true hero.
The fire of the East into the coals of the West!
(He throws the Ecidemon in the fiery glow, and it blazes wondrously. He then turns to Parzival)
Now fit the sword!

Parzival:

As you command!
(He fits together the pieces of the sword.)

Trebuchet:

There, go to the cave's pure spring and dip
the metal in!
(Parzival goes and returns with the whole sword.)
Give it here! So quickly
I'll forge the steel in Ecidemon's fire. *(hammers)*

The morning flows into the heart of evening!
The evening's hue makes whole the dawn!
The body is redeemed, for it is forged
to holy diamond's everlasting hardness.
For the Word is become Flesh: full
of the Grace that comes from the dove
and the Truth that comes from the serpent's light.
Take it, Parzival! And whatever you strike
with this sword, it will never break. Never!

Parzival:

I thank you, Master!
As I once stood defenseless
before you, star-strewn hero,
given o'er to the greatness of your heart

so now you stand there, shorn of your power
before me, your brother. And as you then hurled
your sword away, that we might stand as equals
in the battle we still thought to fight—look—
I give this sword to you, in place of the one
you surrendered me, at risk of life.
For all strife between us is no more.
For who on Earth could ever conquer me,
but you? But you are half of my own heart.

Feirifis (*receiving the sword*):

I accept the gift. And offer these jewels
from my dress, and place them as a crown
upon your head. Beloved brother, like you
I now wait in silence.

Parzival (*embraces him*):

Loved, in eternity.

Feirifis:

Known, and loved!

(*Kundry enters, speaks to Parzival.*)

Kundry:

Hail to you, hero. You are called
to the Grail, called to be the guardian
of the magical stone. I bow before you,
for you are to become Grail-King, Master
of the holiest mystery, crown
of humankind. Kneel! Bend your head
to the dust! (*Parzival obeys.*)

Dust are you—Nothing! Lost, and disappeared!
Light are you—All! Raised, and enkindled.
Whole in God, born to eternity,
you were broken in the night of time,
ruined, and destroyed in the wilderness
but now your heart is redeemed from every death.
Follow to the Grail! And know: those called
to the Grail are called to bring another
with them. Choose your companion!

Parzival:

Feirifis,
do you wish to see with me the mystery
of the Grail?

Feirifis:

I do, my brother.

Parzival:

Then, brother, we will go together.

(*to Kundry*)

Thank you, splendid messenger. Lead
us on!

(Kundry begins leading Parzival and Feirifis out. In the darkness that ensues between scenes, Parzival reappears to find a white-clothed woman sleeping—Conduiramur. She wakes; they embrace.)

Scene 16 The Grail Castle: Whitsun Day

The vestibule as in Parzival's first visit. In the candlelight, Amfortas on his bed. To his left, Repanse de Schoie with her maidens, to his right the chamberlain with the Grail Knights.

Repanse:

Come, Holy Spirit! your day is here, o come!
Descend, you dove, Truth's own blessed wings!
Our innermost heart has looked in hope—for you;
our soul's slow flame is rekindled—by you,
and the light of our belief transfigured—in you.
For look—then when the world was founded:
its image was already accomplished in you,
and the pure breath's fulfillment swelled
out of your womb to us from that time on.
You, our Mother, who quiet those who thirst;
your fire is not flame, devouring what it touches

but a well of eternal rejuvenation,
a creative light, an end of all illusions.

Knights:

Redeem us from death!

Maidens:

Awaken us to holy breath!

Amfortas:

Does he still not come? O you last long hours,
how you hesitate, waver, and stand still
as if no bell dare toll the fateful hour.
O time, thou art nothing before God, yet how terrible
to those who are not in Him! O Lord!
Does he still not come?

Repanse:

Patience, beloved brother!

Amfortas:

O, if you knew the meaning of this word! The very marrow
of my blood's consumed. How long
have I lay, waiting? How long, since Kundry rode off?
How call you this day, we're celebrating, now?

Repanse:

Whitsun, the Spirit's day.

Amfortas:

I am burned up; I have
no more spirit-breath. But you, who comes
bearing promise on your soft wings, O lend *him*
wings as well, that with stormy power
he'll come to quench my parched lip's thirst,
and pour out for me that last, most potent drink
—dark Death, for which my languished being yearns.

Repanse:

The measure of your being must fill up
with sorrow; the cup of grief must fill
to overflowing, for God himself is beyond measure.

Amfortas:

I lay long in fire.
But the fire climbs to more than fire,
the heat to coolness, the despair to praise!
O, what takes place in me? Is this then Death?

Chamberlain:

Hark, the bells! The Grail bells are ringing!

Repanse:

Its chiming bids us come to holy office.
Do you not hear it?

Chamberlain:

With powerful blows it fills the firmament.

Repanse:

The heavens open up reverberant before us;
the choirs of the angels ascend and descend.

Chamberlain:

The vaults are rolling, the whole underworld
unbolts itself with the sound of deep voices.

Repanse:

I see Kundry nearing.
Amfortas, raise your eyes! Parzival nears!

Amfortas:

What do you say?

Repanse:

He who saves you, the pure one. Already he ascends.
And following him, the most chaste of women,
whose hands are like flowers. And yet another Lord
ascends the stairs, Feirifis, ruler of the East.

(*goes forward to meet Parzival*)

Repanse:

Be greeted, honored, beloved, Parzival.
My knee, which never bent to any but
to God, shows you honor. Take my cloak;
take my crown!

Parzival (*takes both and lays them to the side*):

To God alone be honor given!

Repanse:

Be greeted, honored, beloved Conduiramur,
purest of all women! Your hands are the heart
and light of my own. You are chosen, henceforth,
to bear the Grail.

Conduiramur:

Let it be with me as is commanded.

Repanse:

Be greeted, honored, beloved, Feirifis,
you holy brother from the realm of dawn.
What is yours, let it be ours as well,
and that which is ours be given to you.

Feirifis:

You speak words that, like arrows, pierce the heart.
Into your pure and pious hands, I place
my entire self; preserve me, Grail Maiden,
for eternal life.

Repanse:

The gates of the Grail Castle open before you.
(*Parzival hurries to Amfortas and kneels down by his bedside.*)

Amfortas:

You come once more, Parzival? What is the reason
for the visit that you make me?

Parzival:

Beloved Uncle, look at me!
I suffer when you suffer, sigh

when you sigh, cry out when you
cry out. For those wounds which you bear
outwardly, Uncle, burn within me
eternally, if God does not still them.
I am as you. I sinned and I fell
and God did raise me, and the voices called me
here to Monsalvasch. And so I ask you,
patient one, you who suffer, what
are we guilty of, what is the reason
for the suffering that lays you out upon
your bed, that you may neither lie nor sit
but only lean in ever renewed pain
that cripples you and makes you wish for death?

Amfortas (*whose countenance grows ever more radiant*):
The suffering I have born has brought me blessedness,
for your words have now brought healing.
It is through pain that we may become blessed.
Glory to the highest! Redeemed are we all!

All:
Healed is the Earth! Redeemed is the world!

Amfortas:
Bow your head, so I may crown you, Brother!
Repanse, place the purple cloak on him!
Blessed be the King, the Guardian of the Grail;
blessed be he, whose heart penetrated the World!
Take once more the sword, that you, as sign, gave
to your brother, so you are well-arrayed for holy office.

Henceforth, I am servant to this, our King.
Repanse, go now and help ready the Feast.

Repanse:
As the bread gives itself to eat;
the wine to drink, so I give—myself.
Follow to the Grail!

(Repanse, Conduiramur, and the maidens exit to the left, Amfortas, Parzival, Feirifis and the knights, to the right. The bed is carried off. The

chamberlain opens the sun-windows to let light in. The ringing of the Grail bells begins again. The curtain opens, and the banquet hall is seen.

On the place where earlier Amfortas' bed and table stood, an altar in the form of a crystal cube stands. The Grail Knights enter the hall from both sides.)

SONG To the Eternal Feast

Left Group:
To the eternal feast the Grail invites us
with its great bells' bronzéd tones.
O come in, brothers, and fill the World-hall,
you who are the spirit's holy sons.

Right:
Decay has ceased; humankind's made whole.
Life rises up, where pale Death has fled.
Humankind now wears the golden crown
that rests, undying, upon its lifted head.

Both:
For what was ruined is made whole again;
and what was lost, returns to us once more.
From within itself, radiance pours out.
as do our songs, from our heart's deep core.
To the Feast! To the Feast!
To the Feast of Consummation!

(They take their places. Parzival enters, accompanied and served by Amfortas and Feirifis, and ascends the stairs to the altar. The curtain is opened by Titurel.)

Parzival:

In your name, the spirit's name, I speak,
for I wish to approach the altar of the world.
I will admit the guilt of humankind, my guilt,
that cast the altar down into the depths
so that it fell into the night of stone,
fell down to Death. Responsible am I for suffering,
for sickness and pain and for the deeds
through which the health and holiness of humanity
was wasted, and, with it, the whole creation's grace.
I am guilty, too, of the suffering of animals,

the plant's need, the stone's cold rigidity
and all death. O, Spirit of the Grail, you
have restored us to wholeness and to holiness.
Be praised, O holy one.

Angel Choir:

We praise you, we who bear the souls of men and women.
We honor you, we who bear the torch of nations.
We extol you, we who bear the origins of ages.
We rejoice in you, we who bear the powers of form.
We jubilate you, we who bear the forces of motion.
We illuminate you, we who bear the sovereignty of
wisdom.
We resound you from the thrones of the will
We sing you from the mountains of light.
We harp you from the spires of Love.

Feirifis (*who has stepped up to the right side of the altar, takes a scroll from out of his breast, which he unrolls and reads*):

This is the book of Ahura Mazdah, who is the fire
of the Sun. Behold:

The great, kingly light of the Sun
the divine light,
I honor!
The praiseworthy
the all-powerful
revealing itself in act;
the strong-glowing
the deed-creating
streaming over all creation
seeing all.

Parzival:

Lay your holy fire on my lips,
that it may burn all falsehood from my mouth;
to eternity lift my speaking tongue
that I may be a true servant of the Word. Behold!

SONG Lay Your Holy Fire

Lay your holy fire on my lips,
that it may burn all falsehood from my mouth;
to eternity lift my speaking tongue
that I may be a true servant of the Word.

(*He steps to the left side of the altar. All rise. Conduiramur, followed by Repanse and the maidens, enters. She carries the Grail, veiled.*)

SONG Song of the Maidens

Mystery, still concealed
In your stone's dusky shine;
Still image, for us, and sign—
Truth soon to be revealed.

For the last time covered o'er
with veils, pure and virginal
but then—awakened for
fulfillment, eternal.

(*Conduiramur places the Grail upon the altar; the women form a half-circle behind it.*)

Parzival (*when all are bowed*):

Let the Grail be offered. In this offering
the whole world is offered. Offered is the body,
offered is the soul, and offered is the spirit.
Offered is the I.
Offered is the human being with all
that is his and hers.
Offered is each creature that walks upon the Earth,
each that swims in waters, each that flies in wind and air.
Offered is all that greens and blossoms and grows
and sows seed.
Offered is

what is dead and lies
powerless to move, powerless to sound,
beneath our feet.
Offered is
the All,
offered the stars,
offered is the Angel-Choir, the holy nine-fold
spirit of the divine.
For all of this is our dominion, and we live
in you.
Offered is the Grail!

Amfortas:

In Truth.

Feirifis:

In Truth.

SONG Offered is the Body

All:

Offered is the body,
offered is the soul, and offered is the spirit.
Offered is the I.
Offered is the human being with all
that is his and hers.
Offered is each creature that walks upon the Earth,
each that swims in waters, each that flies in wind and air.
Offered is all that greens and blossoms and grows
and sows seed.
Offered is
what is dead and lies
powerless to move, powerless to sound,
beneath our feet.
Offered is
the All,
offered the stars,
offered is the Angel-Choir, the holy nine-fold
spirit of the divine.
For all of this is our dominion, and we live
in you.
Offered is the Grail!

Parzival:

May the offer be accepted! All returns
to You! In eternity, let the Grail
be revealed.

(*He reveals the Grail.*)

Parzival:

Your light transforms all Death to Life.
Thus saith the Word: I am.

SONG May the Offer Be Accepted

May the offer be accepted!
All returns to You!
Your light transforms
All death to life.
Thus saith the Word, I am!

finis

About the Author

DANIEL POLIKOFF earned his Ph.D. in Comparative Literature from Cornell University. After completing his graduate degree, interest in Rudolf Steiner's work led him to pursue studies in anthroposophy and Waldorf education at Sunbridge College in Spring Valley, New York and at Rudolf Steiner College in Fair Oaks, California, where he completed his formal training as a Waldorf high school teacher. Mr. Polikoff has been a guest teacher at the Toronto (where he taught Parzival), Kimberton, and East Bay Waldorf high schools. He currently teaches in Rudolf Steiner College's San Francisco Waldorf Teacher Education Program.

In addition to his Waldorf teaching, Daniel Polikoff is a Rilke scholar and translator as well as a poet. He has published translations of Rilke as well as his own poetry in literary journals such as *The Chariton Review, The Louisville Review, Nimrod,* and *Phoebe*. He is currently at work on a book on Rilke. Mr. Polikoff lives with his wife Monika Leitz and their two children in Mill Valley, California.